P9-DDV-419

The
Effective
College President

THE
EFFECTIVE
COLLEGE PRESIDENT

James L. Fisher
Martha W. Tack
Karen J. Wheeler

AMERICAN COUNCIL  MACMILLAN
ON EDUCATION PUBLISHING COMPANY
NEW YORK
Collier Macmillan Publishers
LONDON

The American Council on Education/Macmillan Series on Higher Education

Macmillan Publishing Company
866 Third Avenue, New York, N.Y. 10022

Collier Macmillan Canada, Inc.

Library of Congress Catalog Card Number: 88-5107

Printed in the United States of America

printing number
1   2   3   4   5   6   7   8   9   10

Library of Congress Cataloging in Publication Data

Fisher, James L.
    The effective college president / James L. Fisher, Martha W. Tack,
Karen J. Wheeler.
        p.   cm. — (The American Council on Education/Macmillan series
on higher education)
    Bibliography: p.
    ISBN 0-02-910321-5
    1. Universities and colleges—United States—Administration—Case
studies.   2. College presidents—United States—Case studies.
I. Tack, Martha W.   II. Wheeler, Karen J.   III. Title.   IV. Series.
LB2341.F494 1988   88-5107
378'.111—dc19   CIP

Contents

v

Preface

The college president. A former professor who presides at convocations and faculty meetings, raises money, and creates few waves—a kind of elevated Mr. Chips. This might have been the profile of a college president once, but no more.

The results of the study reported in this book suggest that the effective college president might be quite different from this traditional predecessor. In fact, the effective college president could have more in common with his or her corporate counterpart. And the implications could portend dramatic changes for every segment of the university community: trustees, faculty, staff, and president. In addition to these groups, we hope this book serves as serious food for thought for those who would be college presidents.

In this study, *effective* presidents are identified and then compared with their typical, or *representative*, presidential counterparts to see whether the effective presidents are, indeed, different. Four hundred eighty-five individuals considered knowledgeable about higher education were asked to identify five persons whom they considered the most effective college presidents in the nation. The 485 included administrators of 28 private foundations, 35 scholars of higher education, and more than 400 randomly selected presidents of two- and four-year, public and private institutions.

These "experts" who responded (222) defined the effective president by whatever terms they chose. Out of a possible 3,300 presidents, the experts identified 412 effective presidents. Along with a random sample of representative presidents (those who remained from the original 3,300), the 412 effective presidents were asked to complete a 15-minute questionnaire, The Fisher/ Tack Effective Leadership Inventory. The results *proved statistically significant in differentiating between effective and representative presidents.*

How were effective presidents different? Among other things, when compared with representative presidents, they were found to

- Be less collegial and more distant
- Be more inclined to rely on respect than affiliation
- Be more inclined to take risks
- Be more committed to an ideal or a vision than to the institution
- Believe more strongly in the concept of merit pay
- Be more thoughtful than spontaneous
- Work longer hours
- Be more supportive of organizational flexibility than rigidity

We also found that, although most effective presidents held a PhD, a number did not. In addition, they had more experience in administration and other fields outside higher education than representative presidents and were appointed at a younger age than other presidents. And interestingly, although a number of the effective presidents graduated from Ivy League or Seven Sister institutions, their parents were more likely not to have graduated from high school. Contrary to conventional wisdom, their spouses were less likely to be professional volunteers for the institution. They had published more, and, in the "for what it's worth department," they tended to be members of the American Council on Education and to have graduated from Michigan, Yale, Harvard, or Vanderbilt.

These results fly in the face of traditional thinking about the college presidency. In general, these presidents were not the collegial prototype. They were strong, action-oriented visionaries who acted out of a kind of educated intuition.

Perhaps college and university governing boards and faculties have been looking for the wrong types of persons to lead our colleges and universities. Or, if a good one slips through the selection process, many institutions have become so diffused and bureaucratized that they squelch the dynamism of an energetic president. The answer is probably a bit of both, but, regardless, the results have been unfortunate.

How did we come to this state? Since about the mid-1960s, university governance has become so egalitarian that, in most institutions, no one is really in charge or responsible. During this period faculty and students have begun to pop up everywhere: on board committees and even on governing boards themselves. There has been nothing left about which the still-accountable president could be benevolent. This folksy arrangement has led to all kinds of leaks and no one with enough authority to repair them. University and college governing boards have granted as rights to faculty, students, and staff what presidents had formerly been able to grant as privileges. And, of course, the new egalitarianism has affected the presidential appointment process.

And so it is today. But in this book, we hope to have eliminated some of the mystery and to have challenged many of the historic assumptions about the college presidency today. It is our earnest hope that we have contributed to a legitimate new view about the college presidency: one that assumes, for a moment at least, that the exception should be the rule.

JAMES L. FISHER
MARTHA W. TACK
KAREN WHEELER

Acknowledgments

Without the support of hundreds of people, we could never have completed this book. Although it is impossible to list everyone who made important contributions, we wish to acknowledge several key people.

First of all, we wish to thank Dr. F. David Mathews, President of the Kettering Foundation, and Mr. Herman Smith, Senior Associate with the Kettering Foundation, for arranging our introduction. Had they not insisted, we would not have met at the 1983 American Council on Education meeting in Toronto and could never have worked collaboratively on this book.

Second, we wish to recognize Mr. Robert L. Payton, President Emeritus of the Exxon Education Foundation, for being bold and adventurous enough to fund the project, even over the objections of external critics. Additionally, we appreciate the help and constant support of Dr. Richard Johnson, our Program Officer at Exxon. We are also extremely grateful to Mr. Glegg Watson of the Xerox Foundation for his support during the later stages of the project. We note here that, although the Exxon Education Foundation provided funding for the research, the views expressed in this book are not endorsed by or in any way attributed to the Foundation.

We would obviously be remiss if we didn't acknowledge the tremendous contributions made to the project by Bowling Green State University (BGSU) and, more specifically, the Department of Educational Administration and Supervision (EDAS). We always knew that we would receive needed financial, technical, and moral support. Thank yous are certainly in order to Dr. Leslie Chamberlin, Chair Emeritus of EDAS, for consistently pushing us in the right direction and to Dr. Richard O. Carlson, the current Chair of EDAS, for his commitment of resources and time to the effort. Other people at BGSU to whom we are most grateful include Dr. Jim Sullivan and Dr. Robert Yonker, our statistical consultants; Dr. Jerry Wicks, our survey construction expert; Russ Mayer, our computer programmer; and Chris Anglis, Deb Burris, Marti Smock, Denise Ottinger, and Beth Sweitzer, our "friends in need." We also graciously acknowledge the hard work and dedication of Judy Maxey, Sherry Haskins, and Sheryl Sabo, members of the Word Processing Center in the College of Education and Allied Professions at BGSU. Their concern for perfection and their loyalty in helping us complete this book were our mainstay on numerous occasions.

The staff at the Council for Advancement and Support of Education also contributed volunteer time and energy to the effort. We certainly appreciate Kathy Yealdhall's expert assistance and the finely honed editorial skills of Nancy Raley. We also wish to express our gratitude to Jeff Burnett for being our intermediary on numerous occasions and for keeping us on target.

We also thank Dr. Richard Paulsen and Drs. J. Richard Bryson, William C. Cassell, Paul Olscamp, David H. Ponitz, and Sr. Ann Francis Klimkowski, PH, the five Ohio college presidents who helped us develop our interview guide. In addition, we offer our heartfelt thanks to the 18 presidents who consented to be interviewed as part of our research effort.

Last, without the contributions of the 615 presidents who responded to the Fisher/Tack Effective Leadership Inventory, the 256 presidents who participated in the pilot test of the inventory, and the 222 persons who nominated effective presidents, this study would never have gotten off the ground. We know presidents receive dozens of surveys each week, and we are genuinely thankful to the 615 of them who chose to return ours.

Of course, we thank those "significant others" in our lives for putting up with us during this almost three-year project. Their support made our sleepless nights, full travel itineraries, and generally overwhelming work schedules palatable. Joan Fisher; Jason and Jarrod Tack; Gary Heberlein; Pat, Garland, and David Wheeler—we couldn't have made it without you.

· 1 ·

Presidential Effectiveness: Unexplored and Undefined

> Name a great American college or university, and you will find
> in its history a commanding leader or leaders who held its pres-
> idency. Name an institution with a brilliant but now-withered
> past, however, and you will probably have little difficulty in
> identifying the weak headmen presidents who have blocked its
> progress. Colleges and universities, focal institutions in the life
> of the nation, need especially strong leaders. (Cowley, 1980, p.
> 70)

There is no real question in anyone's mind that strong, effective
leadership, particularly at the presidential level, is essential to
ensure a positive future for higher education today. Moreover,
higher education's ability to make lasting contributions to society
rests on the leadership of presidents who are aggressively com-

1

mitted to developing quality institutions that are financially sound and capable of carrying out their missions.

Every college must have a president, but as Stoke (1959) and Kauffman (1984) note, who the president is certainly makes a difference. Even though the rewards for effective leadership are limited, according to Kauffman (1984), higher education must have exceptionally good administrative leadership to meet the demands placed on it by many constituent groups. Moreover:

> History shows that a college or university might be elevated to a higher level of significance, continue on its traditional course, or begin on a slippery path toward failure as a direct result of the person selected by the board to lead its institution. (American Council on Education [ACE], 1986, np)

In addition to the forthright comments made by Cowley, Stoke, Kauffman, and Gale, dozens of other authors highlight in journals and books the need for effective presidents. Noted authorities have also debated the issue in public forums. Consequently, the message has become so commonplace and repetitious that we often ignore it. In addition, attempts to find ways to ensure strong leadership have failed so frequently that even some of higher education's most faithful advocates have thrown up their hands in dismay, intimating that there aren't any answers, only questions. They argue that there is really no way to determine at the outset who will be an effective leader and who will not.

Naturally, some people attribute a president's effectiveness to blind luck, fate, or being in the right place at the right time. Although luck can be a factor in maximizing a person's or an institution's potential, we began to wonder if effective presidents create their own luck through use of a special leadership style and philosophy that are different from those of typical presidents. Given the imperative to know more about effective leadership, we decided to do something about the existing information void. So, with the financial support of the Exxon Education Foundation and the resource contributions of Bowling Green State University, we conceptualized and implemented a nationwide study to identify the characteristics of effective college presidents. Indeed, funding such a controversial project was risky for the Foundation. But, as our research confirms, boldness is an essential ingredient in successful leadership.

After reviewing other research regarding the characteristics of an effective college president, we found that most of the information available about presidents relates to identifying their roles and functions and to the relationship that should exist between the president and his or her board of trustees (Kerr, 1984). In addition, data are available about presidential profiles (Bolman, 1965; Cohen & March, 1986; Ferrari, 1970), presidential selection procedures (ACE, 1985; Nason, 1984), presidential evaluation (Fisher & Quehl, 1984; Nason, 1980), the concept of leadership and ambiguity (Cohen & March, 1986), the use of power in the presidency (Fisher, 1984a), and a variety of other functional themes. Moreover, there are a few studies on effective institutions (Astin & Scherrei, 1980; Gilley, Fulmer, & Reithlingshoefer, 1986; Whetten & Cameron, 1985).

Despite the existence of many position papers on presidential effectiveness, only limited empirical evidence is available about the topic, and most of it relates to the management style used by 2-year college presidents (R. G. Gardner & Brown, 1973). We did find one noteworthy study, completed by Pruitt in 1974, that served as the prototype for this effort. Pruitt's pioneering work with 25 presidents generated some interesting conclusions about the personal and professional characteristics of effective chief executive officers. Although there were trait and background differences between his 25 presidents and presidents at large, Pruitt did not delve into differences in their leadership behaviors, an area we consider critical to an understanding of leadership effectiveness.

Since Pruitt's study, there has been limited research on the effective college president in any setting. In 1981, Benezet, Katz, and Magnusson explored the intricacies and human dynamics of the presidency. In completing their project, the researchers studied 25 institutions and their leaders. And, more recently, researchers at George Mason University identified and studied 20 institutions of higher education that were deemed innovative and successful. They then drew conclusions about the characteristics of the presidents (Gilley et al., 1986).

DEFINING EFFECTIVENESS

If you ask five people what makes a person effective, you will get five different answers. As Bennis and Nanus (1985) note:

> No clear and unequivocal understanding exists as to what distinguishes leaders from non-leaders, and perhaps more important, what distinguishes *effective* leaders from *ineffective* leaders and *effective* organizations from *ineffective* organizations. (p. 4)

Cameron and Whetten (1983) go on to say that no one agrees on the meaning of the term because "there is no best constituency to define effectiveness. The criteria used by different constituencies to define effectiveness often differ markedly, and spirited debates about which constituency's criteria are most valuable continue in the literature" (p. 270).

Fortunately, several prominent scholars have given us some worthwhile ideas about effectiveness. According to Drucker (1967), effectiveness is doing the right things, whereas efficiency is doing things right. Bennis and Nanus (1985) add that effectiveness is "activities of vision and judgment," and efficiency represents "activities of mastering routines" (p. 21). Other prominent educators and business executives have offered opinions about effectiveness, but existing definitions create ambiguity and leave us with a sense of frustration. We simply have not been able, thus far, to get a handle on the subject.

Why, until now, has there been no investigation using a research population of over 25 subjects focused on defining individual presidential effectiveness? Why have researchers consistently sought out effective institutions rather than individuals to study? Why have academicians been content to accept personal opinion about effectiveness as fact rather than to delve into the topic through use of systematic research techniques? We asked ourselves these questions repeatedly and drew some conclusions.

1. *There is a tendency to say that you cannot separate effective individuals from effective and, in many cases, highly visible institutions.* Some researchers maintain that effective institutions are always led by effective chief executive officers. Thus, if institutional practice is the critical variable, some academicians suggest that it

makes sense to study institutions and draw conclusions about leadership styles from such investigations.

Our research methodology, which at the outset involved the identification of effective presidents rather than effective institutions, is different from that used in previous research on college presidents. This methodology was chosen because we believe it is just as logical to study individuals whose personalities and operating styles dramatically affect an institution's success or failure as it is to study institutions and generalize about the traits of their leaders. As Levinson (1980) points out, it is important to look "more closely at the subtleties of behavior that differentiate those who have significant leadership potential from those who do not" (p. 119).

Although early leadership-trait studies were equivocally received, so were situational leadership studies. Given the fact that statistically significant differences emerged between effective and representative presidents in this study, perhaps we, along with Miller (1983) and Burns (1978), will revive interest in future studies on the characteristics of effective leaders. As Burns notes:

> The study of leadership in general will be advanced by looking at leaders in particular. The development of certain leaders or rulers is described not in order to "solve" leadership problems or necessarily to predict what kind of leader a person might become, but to raise questions inherent in the complexity of the leadership process. (p. 27)

2. *Researchers may hesitate to identify those who are considered highly effective leaders because of the controversy it generates.* Some people believe that such studies represent sensationalism in its purest form. They say that name-recognition studies resemble popularity contests based primarily on the national visibility of the person or the heritage of the chief executive officer's (CEO's) institution. Because no listing of effective leaders is ever exhaustive, some people are inevitably overlooked. And, of course, it's the people not listed who may cause some to disregard the research results altogether. Interestingly, the results of Pruitt's 1974 study of 25 effective presidents were never published, even after repeated attempts on the part of the author, because of the highly volatile nature of the findings and the reluctance of editors to become associated with the research effort.

To reduce the effects of such factors, nominations were requested from people in virtually every state and in every type of institution in the United States. Moreover, we asked hundreds of people, representing a broad array of positions from current presidents to private foundation heads, to help identify the sample population. Many of the 222 people who took part in the nomination process began their responses with words such as "It is almost impossible to identify only five effective presidents in the nation because there are so many presidents from whom to choose. However, after careful consideration, I submit the following names." Thus, on the basis of conversations and correspondence with several respondents, we believe they took seriously the request to nominate effective presidents, and we contend that the nomination process was a meaningful exercise.

3. *Perhaps people have been unwilling to tackle the problem of defining effectiveness because it resembles trying to find an answer to the age-old question "How do you identify a moral or just human being?"* Like pre-platonic philosophers, some scholars have argued that everything (morality, virtue, and effectiveness included) is relative. In keeping with this notion, Jenkins (1947) suggests that leadership is situational and, thus, that conducting research regarding common characteristics of successful leaders is an exercise in futility. Fortunately, Stogdill (1948) retorts that there is value in such studies:

> Must it then be assumed that leadership is entirely incidental, haphazard, and unpredictable? Not at all. The very studies which provide the strongest arguments for the situational nature of leadership also supply the strongest evidence indicating that leadership patterns as well as non-leadership patterns of behavior are persistent and relatively stable. (p. 65)

However, Stogdill also notes that studies of leadership traits are frequently fraught with methodological problems and, as often as not, produce weak and inconclusive findings.

Unfortunately, almost 40 years have passed since Stogdill suggested that research on the topic could be valuable. And it has been almost 30 years since Selznick (1957) said that there might be some "distinguishing personal traits or capacities" (p. 22) that set leaders apart from followers. However, we still have no concrete data to use in determining who will be effective leaders and who will not be. We concur with R. L. Katz (1974), who says, "Although the selection and training of good administrators is widely recognized as one of American industry's most pressing problems, there is suprisingly little agreement among executives or educators on what makes a good administrator" (p. 23).

As we thought about the value of our research, we remembered Cox's (1985) story about what he learned from Miss Curtis, his fifth-grade mathematics teacher. As Miss Curtis postulated, "All squares are rectangles, but all rectangles aren't squares. The message from this lesson was that while squares are worthy of our special attention, rectangles are a more complex subject" (p. 105). So it is with effectiveness: Studies of presidents in general are worthwhile, but the study of effectiveness in the presidency, although complex, is warranted, legitimate, and exciting.

We believe the results of this 2-year study are especially important today in an environment characterized by confusion, uncertainty, and eroding public confidence in higher education. Boards search for chief executive officers who can provide leadership, and faculties as well as students seek guidance as they pursue excellence in teaching, research, and service.

Given these conditions, those of us concerned about the future of higher education can benefit from knowing more about the personal characteristics, professional attitudes, and leadership behaviors that enhance presidential effectiveness. Specifically, the information gathered should be useful to practicing presidents who are interested in being more effective, to persons who aspire to a presidency, to board members responsible for selecting the pivotal leaders for their campuses, and to faculty in higher education administration preparation programs as they screen and train leaders. And, of course, those interested in learning more about general leadership principles should benefit from the availability of such information.

OUR RESEARCH METHODS

To identify the factors that contribute to presidential effectiveness, we completed a four-phase research study. The study, which began in the fall of 1984, involved identifying a cadre of 412 persons deemed by their peers and associates to be effective presidents; selecting a stratified random sample of 412 presidents who were not included in the nominated group; developing, pilot testing, and refining a survey instrument; disseminating the instrument to 824 chief executive officers; and individually interviewing 18 people who were among those nominated most frequently in the four sectors of higher education (2-year, 4-year, public, and private). In each phase of the study, we made a special effort to ensure the objectivity of data collected.

Before describing the intricacies of our research effort, we need to establish definitions for some of the major terms used. *President* is a generic label for any individual (president, chancellor, dean, or superintendent) responsible for leading a single campus or a multi-campus system with degree-granting authority in postsecondary education. This permits us to use one term rather than the variety of titles used from state to state according to board preference. When we refer to *effective* presidents, we mean the 412 presidents nominated by their peers and associates. When we use the term *representative,* we describe the stratified random sample of 412 presidents who were not nominated.

Phase I: Identifying the Research Population

In developing the methodology for this study, we ran into a major dilemma: How should we identify our effective presidents? Using Stogdill's 1948 categorization, we found that there are five basic ways to identify and study the personal characteristics of leaders: (1) Observe the individual's behavior in a group setting; (2) have associates vote for individuals with certain traits; (3) have qualified observers nominate or rate people; (4) select leaders occupying a particular position and then rate or test them; and (5) analyze case histories and biographical data. After discussing the pros and cons of using each of these procedures, we decided to identify the effective segment of the research population by combining the two following relevant methods:

1. *Voting by Associates.* Because we believe that the opinions of colleagues and peers are worthwhile, we involved leaders, or other current presidents, in the nomination process. Presidents interact frequently and know the problems and issues an effective president faces; therefore, they can competently assess the existing population of chief executive officers and isolate those they consider effective. Incidentally, Maslow (1970), in his study of the self-actualized person, used trusted associates to identify the persons he studied.

2. *Nomination by Qualified Observers.* Given the fact that many external organizations influence higher education, it seemed logical to involve qualified observers in the nomination process. We believe funders, heads of major national higher education professional associations, and scholars of the presidency have the backgrounds needed to make intelligent judgments.

Consequently, we asked 485 people with expertise and experience in higher education to identify the five people they considered to be the most effective college presidents in the nation. (See Table 1.1 for information about the nominators.) These 485 persons included 78 qualified observers and 407 associates. In the qualified-observer arena, we included the following people: heads of 15 major national higher education professional associations (members of the Washington Secretariat); heads of the 28 private foundations that gave the most money to higher education institutions in 1983; and 35 scholars who had written articles, books, or both about the presidency between 1979–1984. The 407 associates included current presidents of 2-year, 4-year, public, and private institutions of higher education in the United States.

In selecting the 407 associates (presidents and chancellors) to be involved in the nomination process, we used a pool of 2,800 rather than 3,300 American institutions of higher education. The 500 colleges that were eliminated fell into two distinct categories: proprietary or profit-making institutions and colleges designated in the 1984 *Higher Education Directory* as professional or specialized (law, medicine, and theology). We assumed that those who head these highly specialized colleges have limited interaction with presidents in other types of institutions. We felt this factor might compromise their ability to nominate effective presidents other than those from similar institutions.

After eliminating these 500 institutions, we grouped the institutions into nine geographical regions and four sectors (2-year, 4-year, public, and private). Using the 1984 *Higher Education Directory* and a table of random numbers, we identified the 407 nominators. As can be seen in Tables 1.1 and 1.2, the total pool of nominators proportionately represented every sector of higher education and every region of the country. By using a nationwide group of nominators, we felt that individuals from throughout higher education had an equal opportunity to be identified.

After much thought and discussion, we decided not to share any preconceived definition of the term *effective* with the people who were asked to nominate presidents. Because the research effort was focused on defining effectiveness in terms of characteristics and styles, we did not want to place restrictions on the nominators or insert personal biases. If, through this process, sig-

Table 1.1
NOMINATING SAMPLE BY CATEGORY

CATEGORY	NUMBER INVOLVED	NUMBER RETURNED	%
Qualified Observer			
Professional association head	15	8	53
Private foundation head	28	16	57
Scholar	35	14	40
Subtotal	78	38	49
Associate			
4-year public president	83	37	45
4-year private president	160	74	46
2-year public president	142	68	48
2-year private president	22	5	23
Subtotal	407	184	45
Total	485	222	46

nificant differences emerged, we thought the results might be even more important.

After one follow-up effort, nominations were received from 222 (46%) of the participants (Table 1.1), which resulted in the identification of 415 presidents. In finalizing the list, we removed the names of three people who operated statewide governing, coordinating, or advisory boards because their positions did not fit the previously established definition of a president. The nomination process consequently resulted in identifying 412 effective college presidents to be involved in other phases of the research effort.

This number (412) represents approximately 15% of the 2,800 college presidents eligible for the study. In terms of frequency of identification, 252 presidents were nominated only once, whereas 160 people received multiple nominations (at least two votes). Specifically, 65 presidents received two nominations, and 95 CEOs received three or more nominations. Although some presidents were identified only once, the most frequently nominated president was identified by 50 different individuals. As noted in Tables 1.3 and 1.4, the 412 presidents represented every sector of higher education, with the greatest number coming from 4-year private institutions.

Simply identifying the personal and professional backgrounds

Table 1.2
NOMINATING SAMPLE BY REGION

REGION	NUMBER INVOLVED
Northeast	42
Mid-Atlantic	79
South Atlantic	94
East South Central	29
East North Central	81
West North Central	51
West South Central	35
Mountain	20
Pacific	54
Total	485

and the salient components of leadership behavior for effective presidents would have been hollow without a comparative base. Therefore, we also included in the study a stratified random sample of 412 presidents who were not nominated by their peers and associates as being effective. In identifying this group, we removed the names of the effective presidents from our previously established master list of 2,800 presidents throughout the country and grouped the remaining 2,388 presidents by region and the type of institution at which they worked (2-year, 4-year, public, and private). Using a table of random numbers, we selected 412 people for the comparative group. The composition of the effective and comparative groups is described in Table 1.4.

Phase II: Developing and Distributing the Survey Instrument

When this study was initiated in 1984, there were no instruments available to use in identifying the distinguishing characteristics of effective college presidents or CEOs in the business and industrial sector. Therefore, we needed a data-gathering device. Given the importance of the instrument to the validity of the research study, we exercised special care in developing the Fisher/Tack Effective Leadership Inventory. Because we were interested in demographic differences between effective and representative presidents, two sections of the instrument contained questions about the individual's personal background. However, the focal

Table 1.3
DISTRIBUTION OF EFFECTIVE AND REPRESENTATIVE PRESIDENTS

SECTOR OF HIGHER EDUCATION	EFFECTIVE	REPRESENTATIVE	TOTAL
4-year public	120	76	196
4-year private	183	165	348
2-year public	106	145	251
2-year private	3	26	29
Total	412	412	824

point of the instrument was the section on leadership attitudes and behaviors.

In an effort to keep the questionnaire short, we decided that ultimately we wanted to include no more than 40 items related to attitudes and styles of leadership. To end up with this predetermined number of items, we developed 109 statements that dealt with a variety of issues ranging from the use of power to social relationships (appendix A).

We then distributed the statements to a stratified random sample of 400 college presidents. Once again, this population of presidents was stratified by institutional sector and geographical location, in an effort to assure a proportionate distribution of respondents. Using the 1984 *Higher Education Directory,* the 2-year, 4-year, public, and private institutions were identified for each region of the country. After establishing proportional limits for each region and for each sector within the region, we used a table of random numbers to make the final selections. As noted in Table 1.5, the initial mailing and one follow-up effort elicited 256 (64%) responses from the survey population.

Table 1.4

EFFECTIVE AND REPRESENTATIVE PRESIDENTS BY REGION

	EFFECTIVE				REPRESENTATIVE				TOTAL
	4-Year		2-Year		4-Year		2-Year		
	Public	Private	Public	Private	Public	Private	Public	Private	
Northeast	7	24	6	1	5	14	7	2	66
Mid-Atlantic	23	34	8	0	11	31	20	5	132
South Atlantic	23	35	20	1	14	26	27	5	151
West South Central	11	16	8	0	10	11	13	2	71
Pacific	10	19	18	0	5	22	26	1	101
Mountain	1	1	7	0	6	3	9	1	28
East South Central	11	13	3	1	6	6	11	3	54
East North Central	17	25	21	0	11	30	21	4	129
West North Central	17	16	15	0	8	22	11	3	92
Total	120	183	106	3	76	165	145	26	824

Table 1.5
PILOT-TEST PARTICIPANTS

Region	4-Year Public			4-Year Private			2-Year Public			2-Year Private			Total		
	Number Involved	Number Returned	%	Number Involved	Number Returned	%	Number Involved	Number Returned	%	Number Involved	Number Returned	%	Number Involved	Number Returned	%
Northeast	5	2	40	17	9	53	7	4	57	3	1	33	32	16	50
Mid-Atlantic	10	3	30	28	18	64	15	8	53	4	2	50	57	31	54
South Atlantic	14	8	57	26	16	62	26	20	77	2	1	50	68	45	66
East South Central	6	5	83	9	5	56	10	8	80	3	1	33	28	19	68
East North Central	7	7	100	28	15	54	30	18	60	3	2	67	68	42	62
West North Central	9	5	56	19	16	84	13	10	77	3	1	33	44	32	73
West South Central	11	8	73	12	8	67	13	7	54	1	0	0	37	23	62
Mountain	6	5	83	4	3	75	9	7	78	1	0	0	20	15	75
Pacific	7	5	71	12	9	75	26	19	73	1	0	0	46	33	72
Total	75	48	64	155	99	64	149	101	68	21	8	38	400	256	64

Reducing the number of statements to be included in the final instrument was a twofold process. First, 49 (45%) of the original 109 statements were eliminated on the basis of comments from respondents that the items were confusing, ambiguous, or problematic. Then, through factor analysis, five factors containing 40 statements were identified. The five factors were labeled the *management style index,* containing 18 statements; the *human relations index* containing 8 items; the *image index* composed of 4 items; the *social reference index* containing 7 statements; and the *confidence index* consisting of 3 items. (See appendices B and C for information related to the five factors included within the instrument.)

Next, we identified the demographic items to be included. After reviewing previously developed questionnaires and U.S. Census Bureau instrumentation, we decided to collect information in the following categories:

1. *Professional Data.* Degrees earned, previous experience, current position, and scholarly activity.

2. *Personal Information.* Age, sex, race, religious preference, marital status, number of marriages, spouse's occupation, number and ages of children, state or foreign country of birth, political affiliation, state of current residence, father's and mother's education, and number of siblings.

The instrument (appendix D) was then printed and distributed to the survey population (412 effective and 412 representative presidents) in December 1985, along with a cover letter explaining the study's purpose (appendix E). Because we didn't want to influence the number of returns from the individuals included in the comparative group, we didn't reveal which presidents had or had not been nominated. After two follow-up rounds, we concluded the survey effort with a 75% response rate (615 questionnaires). In the effective category, 312 presidents, or 76% of the individuals surveyed, responded, as compared with 303, or 74%, of the representative chief executive officers. Table 1.6 contains additional information about the respondents.

Table 1.6
COMPOSITION OF RESPONDING POPULATION

Category	4-Year Public			4-Year Private			2-Year Public			2-Year Private			Total		
	Number Involved	Number Returned	%	Number Involved	Number Returned	%	Number Involved	Number Returned	%	Number Involved	Number Returned	%	Number Involved	Number Returned	%
Effective	120	92	77	183	129	71	106	88	83	3	3	100	412	312	76
Representative	76	68	90	165	106	64	145	112	77	26	17	65	412	303	74
Total	196	160	82	348	235	68	251	200	80	29	20	69	824	615	75

Phase III: Setting Up and Conducting Interviews

To be as exhaustive as possible in approaching the topic of effectiveness, we interviewed 18 people considered to be among the nation's most effective presidents. We thought that interviewing these outstanding individuals might provide some additional insight into the subject of presidential prowess and leadership style.

The 18 presidents were identified by the frequency of their nomination in Phase I of the study, as well as by the sector of higher education they represented. Interviews were conducted with five persons in each sector, with one exception: 2-year private institutions. We interviewed only three people in this sector because of its proportionally small size and the fact that only three presidents from this sector were identified more than once.

We contacted 21 persons in order to schedule the 18 interviews. All of the presidents initially contacted in the 4-year public, 2-year public, and 2-year private sectors agreed to participate in the 2-hour, campus-based interviews. Eight presidents in the 4-year private sector were contacted before 5 persons agreed to participate. The 3 presidents who declined did so for many reasons, including time constraints and lack of confidence in the results of perceptual research. The 18 presidents who consented to be involved in this phase of the research effort included 17 males and 1 female.

We developed an interview guide that focused on specific administrative issues such as the role of the president and the board of trustees, personal habits, and thoughts about what made the individual so effective as president. The interview guide was pilot tested with five college presidents in Ohio. Before this exercise, each president received a copy of the interview guide with the request that she or he review the document and suggest specific improvements. We involved one president from a 4-year public institution, two from 4-year private institutions, and two from 2-year public colleges. Based on the pilot-test results, we added a section on mentoring and reworded questions that seemed awkward. The final interview guide is shown in appendix F.

From October 1985 until August 1986, we interviewed the

selected presidents. These 18 presidents were guaranteed that they would have the opportunity to review any comments attributed directly to them in our publications or presentations and that any other comments would remain anonymous.

The interview tapes were then transcribed and verified. Each tape was reviewed in its entirety, using sophisticated sound equipment in an effort to assure accurate transcription. Portions of the interviews were then used to develop a profile of effectiveness, as included in chapter 5.

Phase IV: Analyzing Data

Finally, we tried to determine significant differences between the responses of effective and representative presidents (2-year, 4-year, public, and private) in terms of demographic characteristics and their styles of leadership. When deemed appropriate on the basis of the nature of the questions and the number of groups compared, we used analyses of variance, t tests, and chi-square as statistical tools. (See appendix G for detailed information about the statistical analyses.)

The analyses of the survey results were reviewed to determine if there were any statistically significant findings. We also looked for patterns of responses in areas in which there were no statistically significant differences.

SUMMARY: THE CASE FOR RESEARCH

Today, institutions of higher education are in desperate need of effective leadership, but there are few individuals who have the characteristics necessary to lead rather than just manage. If, in fact, higher education is to continue performing a vital societal function, leaders who are visionary and unafraid to take risks must be identified to head the institutions of the future.

Naturally, gaining acceptance for the idea that there are certain presidents who have the potential to be successful wherever they go, in terms of institutional advancement, will take a great deal of time and involve further research. We believe that our findings are one step in the right direction: They show that there are differences between effective and representative presidents. These differences include personal backgrounds, as well as leadership behaviors and attitudes.

Perhaps information about the factors that contribute to presidential success will encourage some people who might not otherwise have considered a presidency to do so and cause others to rethink their decision to seek a presidential position. Also, the availability of such information should help those involved in the presidential selection process to hone in on specific personal and stylistic traits. Moreover, faculty in higher education administration preparation programs will know the characteristics considered necessary to serve effectively as a campus chief executive officer. They, therefore, can screen prospective students accordingly. Subsequently, higher education and society will reap significant benefits.

Through the following interpretative text, we will highlight our research findings and offer our thoughts about why certain variables were significant and others were not. In chapter 2, the ideas of individuals who have conducted research about leadership practices of effective chief executive officers will be presented, compared, and contrasted. In chapter 3, we will share our research results regarding the personal and professional characteristics of effective presidents. We will also integrate the work of other researchers into our discussion, as we highlight differences and similarities. Chapters 4 and 5 contain what we consider to be significant and new information about effective college presidents. Chapter 4 covers the leadership behaviors of effective presidents. Chapter 5 provides additional insight about presidential effectiveness, based on information gleaned from interviews with 18 presidents who are among the most widely acclaimed in the nation. In the final section of the book, chapter 6, we will share our thoughts about what we found and the impact these findings might have on higher education.

·2·

Research on the Characteristics of Effective Leaders

What does past research tell us about the characteristics of effective leaders? To find out, we reviewed numerous journal articles and scores of books. Once we had read the limited information focused on effective presidents in postsecondary education, we delved into literature available about corporate executives. We thought the overt concern for productivity in business and industry might have spurred research about the characteristics of executives heading profit-oriented enterprises. We also felt that awareness of significant research results about corporate leaders might help us understand the factors contributing to effectiveness in the college presidency.

Because our study related exclusively to campus presidential effectiveness, we limited our information search to the arena of executive leadership. It is possible, of course, that many characteristics of the effective chief executive are found in people holding other administrative positions. However, we didn't want to

21

generalize about people in all leadership positions but to focus only on the characteristics of effective presidents.

What we found was that, as is the case in higher education, most of the studies of effectiveness in the corporate sector focused first on identifying the characteristics of successful organizations. Then the researchers drew conclusions about the individuals holding the chief administrative positions within those particular organizations (Peters & Waterman, 1982; Whetten & Cameron, 1985). These and numerous other studies assumed that good leaders create good organizations; therefore, if you want to study effective leaders, you can do so by using pre-established criteria to identify organizations considered to be effective. Although we were interested in presidential rather than organizational effectiveness, we carefully considered the results of investigations in which characteristics of effective chief executive officers (either presidents in higher education or in the corporate sector) emerged.

WHAT WE LEARNED

Here is what researchers in both higher education and business and industry had to say about what characterizes effective presidents.

They have vision. For some people, the term *vision* has pejorative connotations. It makes them think of religious leaders sitting cross-legged awaiting some sign from a superior spiritual being about the direction they should take. Perhaps people with such a mystical view would say that the college president is a conduit who merely implements the will of the faculty. Naturally, there are those who equate being a visionary with being a fortune-teller. These people would agree with Thwing (1926), who suggests, tongue-in-cheek, that a president must have "the vision of a seer and the voice of the prophet" (p. 135).

Of course, neither of these extreme attitudes reflects current wisdom. Hundreds of writers have maintained that having vision means having some notion about what should be done to maximize the potential of an organization. Some authors call it inspirational vision (Whetten, 1984). Others refer to it as owning a dream (Greenleaf, 1977), exercising creativity (Pruitt, 1974), being opportunity conscious and having visionary intelligence (Gilley et al., 1986), being idealistic (Weathersby, 1973), and demonstrating creative imagination (Prator, 1963).

Although emphatically underscoring the importance of visionary leadership, Fisher (1984a) and Peters and Austin (1985) assert that having an achievable or empowering vision and passionately communicating it to others is more important than the substance of the vision. Kotter's 1982 research yielded similar results. He concludes that effective leaders begin their jobs with overall ideas (concepts) rather than with concrete plans. However, Kotter notes that, during the first 6 to 12 months, the 15 executives he studied focused their attention on developing a specific agenda designed to move the organization forward.

Thus, we see that leaders must stand for something and have some idea about where the enterprise is going. The specifics will evolve, but, as Greenleaf (1977) says, "the dream must be there first" (p. 16) if there is to be true leadership. Perhaps Peck's (1983) words best sum up the importance of vision to successful presidents. He describes the 19 small-college presidents he studied as having "their eyes focused on the pot of gold: a clear sense of what their institutions are, what they ought to be doing, where they are headed, and what they are to become" (p. 18).

The concept of transforming or transformational leadership also embraces thoughts about possessing a dream or having a futures orientation (Bass, 1985; Burns, 1978; J. W. Gardner, 1986a). Basically, researchers use the terms *transforming, tranformational,* and *innovative* interchangeably to refer to "leadership that goes beyond merely managing the system to helping the system achieve its next stage of evolution" (J. W. Gardner, 1986a, p. 23).

Clearly, effectiveness and vision are inextricably intertwined. Leaders, specifically presidents, cannot expect to be effective unless they possess ideas about what the institution should look like in the future and then use other personal and professional skills to move people along the charted course. Without vision there is no evident challenge; no real prospect for achievement; and no overt, compelling need for people to follow. It is apparent, then, that those who have and passionately communicate their ideas shape the future for higher education or business and industry and enhance their own effectiveness.

/ *They have a high energy level.* Endless energy, limitless enthusiasm, and persistent dedication to the task at hand enable effective presidents to work long hours pursuing a dream or a vision. They require stamina and dedication to the job unparalleled in others. Most effective presidents marry their jobs and, thus, are willing to spend inordinate amounts of time either working or thinking about their responsibilities. Perhaps as McClelland and Burnham (1976) suggest, effective leaders can put in such long hours because they enjoy their work and use the discipline of work as an outlet. Wells (1980) confirms this fact when he says, "My whole being was concentrated in this work; yet like any great opportunity, it was so challenging that extraordinary effort was not only possible but exhilarating. The refreshment received in turning from project to project dispelled the tedium" (p. 134).

We have evidence from Cohen and March (1986) and Kotter (1982) that presidents and business executives (general managers) work *on average* about 60 hours a week. Therefore, it is safe to assume that effective leaders "have fun doing what they're doing" (Peters & Austin, 1985, p. 289), or they could not handle the long hours and maintain such a high level of enthusiasm for the job. However, Gilli (1976) cautions us not to equate time at work with effectiveness, because, as he says "requiring an inordinate amount of time may also be symptomatic of an inefficient executive" (p. 30).

As we think about the relationship between energy and effectiveness, Lowell's (1938) words of caution (and idealism) should remind us to keep things in perspective. He suggests that the president "should never feel hurried, or have the sense of working under pressure, for such things interfere gravely with the serenity of judgment that he should always retain" (p. 19). Sammartino (1982) goes so far as to suggest that presidents should limit their work week to a maximum of 55 hours, spending the remaining time in complete leisure. Presidents today probably can't internalize this advice because of many factors, including increasing governmental regulation and accountability. But they do need to remember the importance of maintaining some personal and professional balance in their lives so they can be effective and maintain their sanity.

So, we can say without equivocation that effective leaders give everything it takes to their jobs. They will do anything they can to enhance the potential for organizational and individual success, including making personal sacrifices to achieve the common good. Perhaps, as Robinson (1986) suggests, "leaders are and should be superhuman" (p. 2).

They are visible. Naturally, because of their position, all presidents have responsibilities that take them into the public domain. They make speeches to on- and off-campus groups, and they interact frequently with individuals representing various interest groups. However, there is a difference between being visible and being "in public." Think about any large-group event that you attended recently. There could have been hundreds of people present, but there are only a few that you remember. We suggest that the few you remember were using their visibility effectively.

Although this will come as no surprise to people who have been studying leadership, according to Gilley et al. (1986), effective presidents are not isolated on the campus but generate support for their dream and engender confidence by being seen frequently both on and off campus. Peters and Waterman (1982) refer to such action as "managing by wandering around" (p. 289). As Mortimer and McConnell (1978) point out "unseen administrators will only become targets of anger and hostility in crises, because unfamiliarity breeds contempt" (p. 166). Cox (1985) adds that executives who stay in their offices all of the time "are making a workstyle decision that is personally stultifying and harmful to the enterprise" (p. 46). And Fisher (1984a) has written at length about the most effective kind of presidential visibility.

On the other hand, Dressel (1981) warns us to keep in check the desire for personal recognition. He says that too much publicity (or visibility) for the president rather than the institution can hurt leaders because it promotes feelings of distrust by constituents. If the president is too visible, faculty and students alike might wonder about his or her motives. In keeping with this idea, Peters and Waterman (1982) admonish executives to be "visible when things are going awry, and invisible when they are working well" (p. 82). Astin and Scherrei (1980) encourage presidents to share credit (and consequently visibility) for successes with others as a means of becoming more effective leaders.

Effective presidents, therefore, recognize that visibility, in appropriate proportions, enhances their effectiveness and engenders confidence in both their institutions and themselves as leaders. Intuitively they know when to be seen and when to maintain a low profile. They also know that through acknowledging the accomplishments of others they enhance their own images and develop constituent loyalty.

They relate well to others. Effective leaders are experts in dealing with people. This might be true because they believe in the worth and dignity of each individual (Kamm, 1982) and because they are deeply concerned about the welfare of the people involved (What Makes Top Executives Tick?, 1983). Gilley et al. (1986) find that effective presidents are "people oriented—caring, supportive, and nurturing" (p. 115). To this list of adjectives, Cox (1985) adds warmth. He says, "Warmth is not only the province of the do-gooders and naive, but also of those top executives who thrive in their jobs" (p. 9). He goes on to equate warmth with "the appetite for showing and being shown acceptance" (p. 9).

The literature emphasizes how necessary it is for effective presidents to be intuitive, compassionate, caring, understanding, and humanistic (Carbone, 1981; Fisher, 1984a; Hesburgh, 1979; Prator, 1963; Wakin, 1985). Perhaps, as Fisher (1984a) notes, effectiveness is not gauged by how you treat the mighty but by how you treat average people. Walker (1981) adds that effective administrators must manage resentments and avoid reprisals, in order to demonstrate concern for the welfare of others. The successful leader, according to Townsend (1985), "sees the best in his people, not the worst; he's not a scapegoat hunter" (p. 52).

Greenleaf's (1977) words appropriately sum up the importance of compassion to success. He says that the great leader

> always accepts and empathizes, never rejects . . . but sometimes refuses to accept some of the person's effort or performance as good enough. Great leaders . . . may have gruff, demanding, uncompromising exteriors, but deep down inside

the great ones have empathy and an unqualified acceptance of
the persons of those who go with their leadership. (pp. 20–21)

Effective chief executive officers must possess superb communication skills in order to know what is going on within the
organization (Wakin, 1985). In his pioneering piece on the college presidency, Thwing (1926) talks extensively about the importance of good interpersonal and communication skills to higher
education CEOs. We must keep in mind that Thwing lived in a
different era when reading his comments that the president must
have "the power of getting on well with men. He is to be free
from cantankerousness" (p. 158), must have tact, and should
emphasize "the merit of his associates rather than his own worth.
He is simply to be a gentleman" (p. 160). In keeping with this
theme, Dressel (1981) and Townsend (1985) emphasize accessi-
bility and listening as key elements in leadership success.

In leading the institution, effective presidents use communication and motivational skills to gain the support of internal and
external constituent groups or coalitions (Whetten & Cameron,
1985). In managing these coalitions, effective presidents do not
become pawns between two kings, or, as Whetten and Cameron
put it, they are not "whipsawed by strong interest groups" (p.
40). Although effective presidents work to secure the support of
various interest groups, they always make responsible decisions
(Whetten & Cameron, 1985).

In concert with this idea, Peters and Austin (1985), as well as
McClelland and Burnham (1976), suggest that we view effective
leaders as coaches who make their subordinates feel strong, thus
enhancing employees' ability to think, perform, and take necessary risks. Perhaps effective leaders are able to motivate others
because "They have their personal ambition under control; they
seem to get their kicks out of seeing their own people succeed"
(Townsend, 1985, p. 52). Townsend goes on to say that effective
leaders often promote from within, which usually has a positive
impact on subordinates' personal and professional motivation to
succeed.

We know that another requisite for leadership effectiveness is
good human relations skills. Effective chief executive officers use
persuasion, intelligence, compassion, and finely honed commu-

nication skills to develop and maintain a trusting environment. Consequently, organizational members tend to work enthusiastically to achieve mutually established goals. Presidents cannot be successful unless they possess good interpersonal skills and the inherent ability to motivate others to achieve their true potential. Higher education is a people business, so leaders must finely hone their people skills if they are to be successful.

They draw respect and admiration. To the foundation of effective leadership provided by good human relations skills, we must add respect, both for others and for self. As Prator (1963) and Fisher (1984a) say, faculty respect and admire effective presidents. This faculty support certainly affects a president's ability to accomplish "the dream." Thwing (1926) and Peters and Waterman (1982) also maintain that respect from associates is critical to success. Pruitt (1974) adds his support for the importance of respect to leadership when he says, "The effective president then is one who can establish himself as a legitimate authority figure universally respected if not universally liked by the subjects of his authority" (p. 86). On the other hand, Laney (1984) emphasizes the importance of demonstrating respect for others, a trait that he maintains the ineffective president lacks.

As we discuss respect, we must confront the question of whether one can be both loved (or liked) and respected. Thwing (1926) says presidents should attempt to "win the feeling and the will of love" (p. 165) from those with whom they work. He also says the president "should always be the best friend to his associates. With them, the terms of association should be of the deepest personal regard" (p. 173). In seeming support of this idea, Pray (1979) argues that the *reasonable adventurer,* a term he considers synonymous with the effective president, tends to be friends with his or her associates. He suggests that the issue is one of degree and maintains that the president should not become a "buddy," thereby suggesting guarded openness.

In sharp contrast, Dressel (1981) cautions about confusing respect with love. He says, "Too many administrators want to be loved. They do well if they are respected as administrators, but they are not then likely to be loved by the faculty" (p. 159). He notes that many former presidents believe in maintaining social and psychological distance, a concept for which Fisher (1984a) argues strongly. In support of this position, McClelland and Burnham (1976) suggest that the leader's need to influence others must take precedence over the desire to be liked.

Although presidents must show a sense of caring deeply for those with whom they work, they must maintain some sense of privacy and be able to deal effectively with loneliness (Greenleaf, 1977). According to Benezet, Katz, and Magnusson (1981), presidents have few close friends. Thwing (1926) suggests that this is often true because presidents do not want to be accused of favoritism. Carbone (1981) even suggests that presidents should not share their personal thoughts and actions with others.

Think about familiarity and privacy as being at either end of a continuum. You will generally find that effective presidents hover near the end labeled *privacy*, but presidents maintain their privacy in many ways. In talking about the fine line between familiarity and aloofness, Fisher (1984a) says:

> Distance means being utterly transparent but always remote. Distance is having a close vice-presidential associate after ten years say, "Yes, he's my best friend and I would do virtually anything for him, but I can't say that I completely know him." Distance is recognizing that a leader is no longer "one of the boys or girls." Distance is being a friendly phantom: warm and genuine, concerned and interested, but rarely around too long or overly involved. . . . Distance balances remoteness with familiarity. The effective leader is both excitingly mysterious and utterly known. Distance is being warm and attentive, open and casual, but never, never really getting off that presidential platform with anyone who knows you as the president. (p. 45)

Fisher (1986) adds that presidents must preserve the legitimacy of the office in order to maintain the respect of those to be led. He notes that "there is a vast difference between conducting yourself warmly and sincerely and behaving as if you are simply a colleague who happens to be president" (p. 17).

Fisher (1984a) is not the first academician to advance the hypothesis that social and psychological distance are important elements in effective leadership. Numerous researchers confirm the positive relationship between distance in leaders and group productivity (Blau & Scott, 1962; Carp, Vitola, & McLanathan, 1963; Cleven & Fiedler, 1956; Fiedler, 1955, 1967; Fleishman &

Peters, 1962; D. Katz, 1973; Richman & Farmer, 1974; Rubin & Goldman, 1968; Shaw, 1965; Shepherd & Weschler, 1955; Stogdill, 1974). Others, like Shepherd and Weschler (1955), point out that there are fewer communication difficulties when leaders maintain social distance.

Thus, we have confirmed from a literary perspective that effective presidents recognize how important it is to have respect rather than popularity in order to be effective leaders. Moreover, effective presidents probably lean more toward privacy than familiarity in dealing with constituents. As we will note later in this chapter, these attitudes dramatically affect a president's style of governance in leading his or her institution.

They are bold decision makers. Effective chief executive officers have the courage, conviction, and inner strength as well as the intelligence needed to make bold and sometimes daring decisions. A long list of distinguished authors echo this theme throughout higher education and management literature. They include Argyris and Cyert (1980), Astin and Scherrei (1980), Bennis and Nanus (1985), Carbone (1981), Cox (1985), Enarson (1984), Fisher (1984a), Kotter (1977), Peters and Austin (1985), Peters and Waterman (1982), Townsend (1985), and Whetten and Cameron (1985). In some contrast, Gilley and colleagues (1986) find that the 20 presidents at "on-the-move" institutions they studied "in most cases were not risk takers" (p. 58). They add, however, that they found "strong evidence of innovation, enterprise, and boldness at the individual level" (p. 116).

In his book, *The Making of the Achiever,* Cox (1985) eloquently states the obvious:

> The components of courage for the executive achiever are willingness to: (1) make him or herself vulnerable; (2) speak one's mind fully in a timely fashion; (3) experiment frequently; (4) make bold decisions; and (5) grab hold of his or her unique strengths. (p. 53)

He maintains that boldness is a critical ingredient in making good decisions as well as the mark of effective executives (or achievers, to use Cox's term). Moreover, Kotter (1977) suggests that we must add prudence to the risk-taking formula. Perhaps you can equate effectiveness with sticking your neck out, picking sides, establishing a position, and staying with that position even when others disagree (Peters & Austin, 1985).

Bennis and Nanus (1985) confirm risk taking as an important component of effectiveness. They say it beautifully: "effective leadership takes risks—it innovates, challenges, and changes the basic metabolism of the organizational culture" (p. 52). They add that this form of leadership requires "courageous patience," (p. 52) which, as Peters and Austin (1985) note is "hanging in long after others have gotten bored or given up; its refusing to leave well enough alone" (p. 415). Whetten (1984) also describes risk taking as "aggressive opportunism," which means actively pursuing opportunities, as well as creating a climate that supports risk taking or, as he terms it, developing a "safe-fail" organizational environment.

According to Dressel (1981), many administrators won't make the hard decisions because they recognize that no decision will be completely acceptable. He also maintains that some presidents fool themselves into thinking that everything is fine and exist in a perpetual state of euphoria, whereas others recognize problems, seek input, and then refuse to take a stand on the issue. Townsend (1985) confirms Dressel's notion that administrators must take risks and be decisive if they are going to be successful. In Townsend's view, many people are ineffective leaders because they insist on having all of the facts before moving ahead. He says, "At some point a good leader with inadequate data will say, 'Ready, fire, aim—and if it doesn't work we'll correct it, but at least the timing is right to start with what we have'" (p. 52).

Bass's (1985) words seem to summarize the importance of bold decision making to effective leadership. He says that the transformational (or effective) leader

> may be less willing to be satisfied with partial solutions, or to accept the status quo, or to carry on as before. He is more likely to be seeking new ways, change for its own sake, taking maximum advantages of opportunities despite the higher risks. (p. 105)

He adds that the inspirational leader must "argue successfully for what he sees is right or good, not for what is popular or is acceptable according to the established wisdom of the time" (p. 17).

They use power well. Although some academicians (primarily faculty) view the use of power in higher education as inappropriate, many widely acclaimed scholars maintain that effective leaders are comfortable with power (Kotter, 1977, 1982). As a matter of fact, Carbone (1981) says that "The creative use of power in stimulating faculty action or in moving ahead despite a lack of faculty support is a quality that separates effective presidents from those who merely occupy the office" (p. 83).

In an effort to remove some negative connotations from the concept, McClelland and Burnham (1976) refer to power motivation not as dictatorial behavior but as "a desire to have impact, to be strong and influential" (p. 103). Moreover, Peters and Waterman (1982) say that effectiveness is "being tough when necessary, and it's the occasional naked use of power. . . . " (p. 82).

Before we proceed, we must identify the different types of power available to CEOs. Using French and Raven's 1959 typology, we see that there are basically five forms of power: coercive, reward, legitimate, expert, and referent or charismatic.

Coercive power involves using threats and punishments to achieve compliance and invites retaliation (Kotter, 1977). Because of its negative and manipulative nature, the use of coercive power is not highly effective in higher education. Therefore, leaders should use it sparingly.

Evidence of reward power is the granting of promotions or bonuses to employees to assure future compliance with the chief executive's wishes. Kotter (1977) suggests that effective leaders frequently do "favors that cost them very little but that others appreciate very much" (p. 130) with the expectation that the recipient of the favor will return the gesture. He says that the general managers he studied "even maneuvered to make others feel that they were particularly dependent on the general managers for resources, or career advancement, or other support (pp. 69–70). Because of financial limitations and other professional restrictions, college presidents generally use reward power subtly through praise or support for a person's promotion or tenure.

As J. W. Gardner (1986b) points out, "Power does not need to be exercised to have its effect—as any hold-up man can tell you" (p. 5). Thus, by being president, the officeholder has legitimate power. A president can use such power effectively as long as constituent group members basically agree with the president and see his or her actions as benefiting the group. Based on his studies, Kotter (1982) suggests that leaders often tried

> to make others feel legitimately obliged to them. . . . by stressing their formal relationships. They acted in ways to encourage others to identify with them. They carefully nurtured their professional reputations in the eyes of others. (p. 69)

Expert power comes with knowing what you are doing. This power form comes from being introduced as an expert or actually becoming one through study and experience. Needless to say, college presidents need to develop their expertise in leadership and management if they are to take advantage of this important form of power. Consequently, we believe it is important for presidents to know about "the literature of higher education and other fields that relate directly to their presidency" (Fisher, 1984a, p. 39). Otherwise, they seriously erode their ability to lead.

Through the use of charismatic, or referent, power, leaders are able to exert tremendous influence on the organization. Although there is no agreement in the scholarly community about the precise definition of the term, J. W. Gardner (1986a) suggests that charisma might exist in "leader-constituent relationships in which the leader has an exceptional gift for inspirational, nonrational communication and the followers' response is characterized by awe, reverence, devotion or emotional dependence" (p. 22). Thus, as Whetten (1984) maintains, charismatic leaders are able to move organizations forward with their innate powers of persuasion.

Bass (1985) considers charisma an essential ingredient in effective, or transformational, leadership because through personal charisma the effective leader "motivates us to do more than we originally expected to do" (p. 20). This ability to motivate others might depend on constituent group members' seeing the charismatic leader as an ideal person, both consciously and unconsciously. Therefore, they are more likely to defer to the wisdom and wishes of the leader (Kotter, 1977). As Fisher (1984a) says, "The leader who combines charismatic power with expert and legitimate power, adding a carefully measured portion of reward power and little or no coercive power, achieves maximum effectiveness" (p. 40).

Bass (1985), although a believer in the fact that charisma greatly enhances the chances for success, quietly notes that it is not an essential ingredient. He maintains that an overdose of charisma could affect a leader's effectiveness as dramatically as a lack of the trait. Agreeing with this notion, Argyris and Cyert (1980) note that "A conveyed sense of commitment, courage, and fairness by average executives can usually compensate mightily for an absence of charisma" (p. x). Townsend (1985) even goes so far as to say that "Charisma is not generally associated with a true leader. . . . It is more associated with the opposite: the corporate politician, who is what is the matter with our country" (p. 52). However, even with these warnings, most authors agree that leaders can use charismatic power effectively and that, without any charisma, the leader will be less effective (Fisher, 1984a).

So, we see that leadership and power are not mutually exclusive. As Burns (1978) points out, "leadership is a special form of power" (p. 12). Indeed, leadership is the ability to influence others to achieve predetermined goals, whereas power is the overarching need to influence others. In describing the relationship between leadership and power, Bittel (1984) states that "leadership is rarely derived solely from power; instead, it tends to generate its own power" (p. 10).

So the question remains, Are effective presidents concerned about power and do they use their power? The answer, perhaps lies in J. W. Gardner's (1986b) statements: "To say a leader is preoccupied with power is like saying that a tennis player is preoccupied with making shots his opponent cannot return. Of course, leaders are preoccupied with power" (p. 5). Effective leaders recognize that they have a great deal of power and thus the ability to "influence other people's behavior and lives" (Kotter, 1977, p. 136). Leaders, however, must not use this power to achieve personal gain nor must they use it impulsively. Effective presidents use self-control, maturity, and wisdom in exercising the power needed to achieve organizational goals.

They have a positive self-image. Successful presidents have high self-esteem, which is reinforced by "inner security, a justified self-confidence in one's competence at the job" (Tead, 1951, p. 123). This sense of personal identity and self-worth engenders respect from constituents and allows presidents to care deeply about others because they feel good about themselves. Self-confidence also enables presidents to stand alone rather than be part of a group (Hesburgh, 1979) and to tolerate the real loneliness that often characterizes the position (Greenleaf, 1977).

Leaders do not achieve this presidential image of confidence and self-worth by chance. As Bass (1985) points out, effective leaders are known to "engage in impression management to bolster their image of confidence, increasing subordinate compliance and faith in them" (p. 40). He also notes that effective leaders are wonderful actors, who recognize that they are always on stage and perform accordingly.

The effective leader's image of confidence is bolstered by repeated successes. Bennis and Nanus (1985) describe this preoccupation with winning as the *Wallenda factor*. Here's how they explain it: "It became increasingly clear that when Karl Wallenda poured his energies into *not falling* rather than walking the tightrope, he was virtually destined to fail" (p. 70). They maintain that effective leaders "don't think about failure, don't even use the word" (p. 69) and that they demonstrate enthusiasm for the tasks at hand because of their inner strength and confidence. Although Whetten and Cameron (1985) agree that effective leaders consistently focus on winning, they stop short of saying that they do not even consider the possibility of failure. Rather, they say that effective leaders have "an innoculation theory of failure. While they avoid taking excessive risks that might be viewed as irresponsible, they have a healthy respect for what can be learned from failure. . . . they, in effect, develop a measure of resistance to failure and are less threatened by its prospects" (pp. 38–39).

Although he agrees that effective leaders believe in winning, Kotter (1982) also says that this "I can do anything" attitude must be kept in perspective. In his opinion, this disease frequently afflicts the strong and successful and leads them foolishly to think they are invincible and can do everything. If not controlled, such a "syndrome can seriously retard performance and hurt the careers of very talented people" (p. 143).

As Stogdill (1948) notes, great leaders typically are not the most modest people. However, you should never view their self-confidence or sense of self-worth as cockiness or self-worship (Bennis & Nanus, 1985), arrogance or coldness (Bass, 1985). Presidents must maintain a mature outlook and control their egos in order to make decisions that advance the dream and the institution.

Successful leaders, then, actually engage in image management, are extremely self-confident, and possess superior expertise, which they demonstrate daily. Because they believe in their ability to get things done, they must constantly work to avoid appearing cold, arrogant, and blind to the aspirations of others. Needless to say, effective leaders focus on winning and do so consistently.

They are trusting and trustworthy. Not only must the members of constituent groups trust the president, but the president must return that trust. J. W. Gardner (1986a) emphatically calls for leaders to build on the concept of trust within the organization. He notes that steadfastness, which he equates with reliability or predictability, is essential to developing a trusting environment. He adds "another requirement is fairness—fairness when the issues are being openly adjudicated but, equally important, fairness in the backroom. . . . Nothing is more surely stabilizing than confidence that the leader is unshakably fair in public and in private" (p. 19).

In keeping with this idea, Argyris and Cyert (1980), Carbone (1981), Greenleaf (1977), Kamm (1982), Walker (1981), and Whetten and Cameron (1985) maintain that trust, a sense of fairness, and dependability dramatically affect leadership effectiveness. Additionally, Stogdill (1948) also suggests that there is a relationship between integrity and eminent leadership. Almost 40 years later, Peters and Austin (1985) underscore Stogdill's comments when they declare that effectiveness and integrity must coexist or constituents might call leaders hypocrites, a perception that certainly would impede rather than enhance leadership ability.

Therefore, it appears that effective leaders use "ethical integrity" (Wenrich, 1980) and honesty to build trust throughout the organization, both in themselves as leaders and in the organization as provider. Good faith and goodwill are hallmarks of these leaders' organizations because they are accountable, predictable, reliable, concerned for equity among individuals, and straightforward in their dealings with others.

They have a sense of humor. What keeps effective presidents going? How do they maintain "optimism in the face of adversity" (Enarson, 1984, p. 26)? Perhaps they don't take themselves too seriously and have a healthy sense of humor (Cox, 1985; Pray, 1979; Townsend, 1985). As Carbone (1981) says, "Keep your sense of humor. Recognize you are not infallible, but don't expect to be" (p. 76). Overall, "Don't be a pompous stuffed shirt" (p. 77).

On the basis of our reading and experiences, we agree that a sense of humor contributes immeasurably to presidential success. A joke or a smile eases tension and stills troubled waters, thus facilitating group interaction without creating overt hostility.

They believe in shared governance but. . . . Literature from business and industry, as well as higher education, indicates that effective leaders believe in seeking advice from people to be affected by various decisions. Kotter (1982) notes that even in the business sector, executives "rarely 'gave orders' in the traditional sense. That is, they seldom 'told' people what to do" (p. 80). According to Wells (1980), "academic administrators need to try to cultivate the ability to lead rather than command. The house of intellect is by nature adverse to orders" (p. 119). Peters and Austin (1985) add that effective executives truly listen to the people in the organization and consider their constituents' views more important than their own.

Effective leaders are politically astute, pragmatic, and skillful bargainers (Whetten & Cameron, 1985) who are receptive to suggestions and ideas (Wells, 1980). Dressel (1981) reinforces the importance of listening but adds that chief executive officers should not always accept or follow advice.

Naturally, effective presidents must recognize that there is a fine line between democratic leadership and shared governance. But there are those who believe an institution of higher education is a pluralistic, political democracy (Epstein, 1974; Walker, 1981) and should be governed democratically (Tead, 1951) rather than hierarchically. However, these authors also recognize that even though administrators serve with the consent of the governed, they have to make decisions, with consensus or not, after appropriate and fair deliberation.

Although others, like Pruitt (1974) and Ryan (1984), suggest that the hallmarks of effectiveness are consensus building and the involving of constituents in institutional governance, they do not advocate a democratic administrative style. In their description of higher education governance patterns, Cohen and March (1986) identify eight metaphors of governance, including the democratic (political) and consensus (chairperson) approach. But they do not suggest that any one pattern is better suited than another to higher education.

Of course, we find the notion that the shared governance pattern is the most appropriate for an educational institution acknowledged frequently in the literature (Corson, 1975; Dressel, 1981; Follett, 1940; Kamm, 1982; Millett, 1962, 1978; Stadtman, 1980). These writers usually call for full participation by faculty in decision making. Even when they advocate this participatory model, however, the authors consistently reinforce the idea that authority and responsibility must remain with the chief executive officer. Fisher (1984a) points out that presidents must constantly seek out expert opinions and weigh the evidence carefully in making the best decisions for their institutions, even if they do not represent consensus. He also notes that "When those who are expected to be led believe that they control the leader, this belief significantly compromises both the leader's position and potential" (Fisher, 1986, p. 17).

Based on their 1980 study of 49 private institutions, Astin and Scherrei conclude that there are four presidential types and five administrative styles. Their four presidential types are the bureaucrat who is viewed as remote, inefficient, and ineffective; the intellectual, considered to be laissez faire in terms of leadership style; the nonauthoritarian egalitarian; and the counselor. They maintain that the counselor-type president is "by far the most satisfied of all the presidential types" (p. 68) and demonstrates humanism through a personal approach to administration.

The administrative styles described by Astin and Scherrei (1980) are humanistic, hierarchical, entrepreneurial, insecure, and task-oriented. They note that task-oriented administrators tend to value in subordinates "support from faculty, scholarship, initiative, influence with those in power, willingness to accept authority, willingness to apple-polish, and cooperation" (p. 78). In turn, task-oriented administrators reward creativity, initiative, professional and technical competence, cooperation, and aggressiveness (p. 79). They suggest that "virtually every trait that defines this type [the task-oriented administrator] seems relevant to effective administration" (p. 79).

In the minds of some, taking charge (or being courageous in decision making) works against shared governance. However, this is not necessarily so. Presidents are in charge and are, therefore, expected to be decisive. They don't exercise this decisiveness in a vacuum or they would erode the trust of constituents to the point that leadership becomes impossible. As Lowell (1938) reminds us, presidents must remember that teamwork and success are synonymous. McClelland and Burnham (1976) go on to say:

> Managers must be interested in playing the influence game in a controlled way. That does not necessarily mean that they are or should be authoritarian in action. On the contrary, it appears that power motivated managers make their subordinates feel strong rather than weak. The true authoritarian in action would have the reverse effect, making people feel weak and powerless. (p. 105)

How, then, do effective college presidents govern? They believe in shared governance (or participatory decision making) but recognize that the ultimate responsibility for making the decisions rests on their shoulders. They understand that there is no such thing as collegial leadership, but they always seek opinions and facts from those to be affected by the decisions. Armed with information from many sources, they make the best decision for the institution and higher education in general. Although this decision might not reflect consensus, it represents the most appropriate course of action for the enterprise.

They believe in the underlying goals of the organization. To lead effectively, people must be completely committed to the primary mission and goals of their organization, an attitude that may be "translated as zeal" (What Makes Top Executives Tick?, 1983, p. 124). In the case of higher education, Kauffman (1984) suggests that chief executive officers must "show they appreciate the essence of colleges and universities and why they were created and supported and esteemed for so many generations" (p. 10). He equates such a commitment with "a calling—that at its best has a spiritual dimension" (p. 10). Pruitt (1974) adds that "effective presidents tend to be missionaries in spirit" (p. 88) who are always interested in advancing the cause of higher education.

Effective presidents are also able to lead because of their understanding of and appreciation for higher education's organizational culture. They must be "sensitive to members' strong allegiance to core cultural values and norms" (Whetten & Cameron, 1985, p. 45) and must use this sensitivity to lead the institution. As Whetten and Cameron further comment, "If new administrators demonstrate a full awareness of and sensitivity to the sacred local values, they can gradually win the trust and confidence of long-time members" (p. 45). We noted earlier, however, that effective presidents do not allow the culture alone to dictate what is to be done. They take action, often in opposition to what consensus demands, but they do so from a platform of constituent trust and confidence. They use their finely honed political skills by

> suggesting new approaches rather than directly assaulting accepted practice as bad, inferior, or unenlightened. They justify their proposed changes in terms of staying in touch with a changing environment, and keeping up with competition, rather than belittling past practice, per se. (Whetten & Cameron, 1985, p. 45)

Effective presidents believe that higher education can and does make a difference to individuals and society. Their commitment to leading their institutions reflects their zeal.

The organization IS the leader. According to Szilagy and Wallace (1980), leadership is one of the most important elements affecting organizational performance. Given this proposition, we believe the CEO is the critical ingredient in the success or failure of any higher education institution or corporation. It is the CEO's empowering leadership that bonds diverse constituents together to achieve common goals. It is in this leader that others find hope for a better tomorrow.

We find it interesting that, on the basis of existing literature, there are more similarities than differences in the characteristics of effective leaders in the corporate and higher education worlds. Although this universality of executive characteristics was not the subject of our current research, we observed the phenomenon and think it is noteworthy.

In talking about the importance of having an effective college or university president, Fisher (1984b) says:

> I am convinced that it will be strong, assertive, and enlightened presidents who will lead us to a new and higher level of contribution in this difficult period for American higher education. It will not be faculty or key administrators, it will not be governments, it will not be education associations or scholars, and it will not be boards of trustees. All are important, but our future rests on the bold, decisive leadership of college and university presidents nationwide. (p. 11)

Perhaps, as Bolman (1965) suggests, we need a "paragon to match the prescribed profile" (p. 21). If we consider Thwing's (1926) sage remarks, we recognize that it takes a very special person to execute the duties of a college president. He maintains that the president

> is to bring agreements out of disagreements, to make fitness from unfitness, to get satisfactions out of dissatisfactions. Raising grapes from thorns and figs from thistles is his function. He is to adjust individualities to the standards of a board, to placate the cantankerous, to influence the proud and the bumptious to work with humility and modesty, and to persuade the crude and the coarse to live in peace with the urbane and the mannerly. (pp. 151–152)

To accomplish these Herculean tasks, Wells (1980) maintains that the president should "Be born with the physical charm of a Greek athlete, the cunning of a Machiavelli, the wisdom of Solomon, the courage of a lion" (p. 147). Dressel (1981) adds that the successful president must be

> approachable, articulate, attractive (in appearance and personality), charismatic, confident, considerate, decisive, deliberate, emphatic, fair, firm, flexible, imaginative, persuasive, rational, reliable, sensitive, self-assured, sympathetic, tactful, and tolerant. In addition to this profusion of adjectives, such

phrases as sense of humility, concern for quality, awareness and acknowledgement of personal and institutional weaknesses, inspires confidence, listens attentively, and morale builder appear frequently. (p. 196)

He warns that applying this list of characteristics to administrators in general (and presidents in particular) could "eliminate the species" (p. 196).

Clearly, what one must bring to the chief executive officer's position in order to be successful is overwhelming. Perhaps the pressures on presidents to be paragons of virtue and the erosion of presidential power have contributed to the problems institutions have in recruiting the "right kind" of people for presidencies.

Given the importance of the president, we must know more about what makes this person an effective leader. If it is possible to describe the effective president in terms of leadership behaviors, maybe we can improve the presidential selection process and, in turn, positively influence the future of higher education.

·3·

Effective Presidents: A Personal and Professional Profile

The college presidency has been the subject of endless conversation, investigation, and analysis in higher education since the beginning of the 1950s. Volumes have been written about the backgrounds and life-styles of the persons who occupy the office, the roles and responsibilities they must assume, and the perceived problems or pleasures of the job. In descriptions of the president, emphasis has been placed on such components as educational background, employment patterns, salary, benefits, age, and occupation of spouse. Studies like those conducted by Bolman (1965), Cohen and March (1986), Duea (1981), Ferrari (1970), Gilli (1976), Kerr (1984), and Vaughan (1986) have certainly provided insight into the characteristics of college presidents, and analysis of these data allows us to determine if the traits have changed or remained relatively stable over the years.

Yet never before (with the exception of Pruitt's 1974 study of 25 effective presidents) has there been any attempt to compare

43

the backgrounds of effective presidents with the characteristics of their representative colleagues. Moreover, until now, there was only speculation about the personal and professional traits that contribute to effectiveness in the presidency. However, using our research results, we can begin to talk more definitively about several personal and professional factors associated with effectiveness in the presidency. (Interested readers should refer to appendix H for information about the responses to questions included in the professional and personal sections of the Fisher/Tack Effective Leadership Inventory.)

PROFESSIONAL BACKGROUND

To determine whether there were similarities or differences in the educational background and work-related experiences of effective and representative presidents, we asked several questions in these two areas. We felt that such information would be useful to a number of people, including presidential aspirants and search committee members. We believe our results, which are not surprising in some areas and are breathtaking in others, will generate much thought and conversation in the academic community.

Types of Degrees Earned

Traditionally speaking, the higher education community has acknowledged a pecking order based on the type of academic degree a person holds. Few would deny that professionals who hold the doctor of philosophy (PhD) degree are held in higher esteem that those who have earned the doctor of education (EdD) degree.

Perhaps the notion that a PhD is "better" has been perpetuated because of the research component typically associated with the degree and its strong roots in German universities, which thrived on empirical investigation. In contrast, the EdD is seen as suitable for educational practitioners, usually in elementary and secondary schools, who, instead of concentrating on theory alone, strive to put theory into practice.

In the past, researchers have verified that few presidents hold

EdDs and that most of those who do are found in 2-year institutions. In addition, studies have found few college presidents with professional degrees in such areas as law, medicine, and theology. Consequently, in the general population of campus leaders, the PhD appears to be the degree of choice; however, the question regarding effectiveness remains. Do effective college presidents also favor the PhD? Are there notable differences when one considers the baccalaureate and master's degrees?

Doctorate

As expected, most effective college presidents report that they hold the PhD, with the EdD surfacing as a distant second. The next most frequently mentioned doctorates are in theology and such other areas as law and medicine. Not surprisingly, representative presidents also mirror this general profile.

When compared to our research results, studies conducted by Benezet and colleagues (1981) and Duea (1981) cite a noticeably higher percentage of presidents holding PhDs than EdDs. On the other hand, research restricted to 2-year institutions reveals a higher number of presidents who hold EdDs (Vaughan, 1986). Perhaps this is true because the 2-year college was initially viewed as grades 13 and 14 of secondary education, thus contributing to the expectation that the practice-oriented EdD is more appropriate for faculty and staff in these institutions than the research-focused PhD.

Master's

McDonagh, Schuerman, and Schuerman (1970) conducted one of the few studies that includes information about the type of master's degree obtained by college presidents. These authors found that, of the 74 presidents who reported holding master's degrees, 74% were in the arts, whereas 24% were in the sciences.

According to our research, slightly less than 50% of the effective presidents mention the master of arts. The next most frequently cited degrees are the master of education, master of science, and theology-related degrees such as master of divinity and master of theology. Our findings also show that, at the master's degree level, the type of degree held by effective presidents is not dramatically different from that of the general presidential population.

Baccalaureate

Over 57% of the effective college presidents (as compared with about 49% of the representative sample) earned the bachelor of arts degree. Interestingly, less than 33% of the effective group holds the bachelor of science degree, whereas approximately 40% of the representative presidents hold the BS degree. Other baccalaureate degrees identified by effective presidents include education, pre-law, and theology. Although not identical, these findings are consistent with McDonagh et al.'s 1970 research results, which indicate that 66% of the 100 college presidents they studied held bachelor of arts degrees, and 30% held bachelor of science degrees.

So what do all these numbers mean? They verify the fact that, when considering academic degrees, there is little difference between presidents in general and those deemed by their peers to be effective. Interestingly, however, effective and representative presidents holding BAs, MAs and PhDs outnumber those with BSs, MSs and EdDs by a ratio of more than two to one.

Institutions Attended

There is a popular assumption that the brightest and best in any field come from Ivy League institutions. The perception is that these institutions possess better faculty, conduct more and better research, and have a history of excellence. But, as has been proven time and time again, assumptions are sometimes inaccurate, so we felt compelled to investigate the educational histories of effective presidents.

Doctoral

Effective college presidents earned doctoral degrees from 80 different institutions, with the largest number having attended the University of Michigan. As noted in Table 3.1, 16 institutions

Table 3.1

INSTITUTIONS GRANTING DOCTORAL DEGREES

INSTITUTION	EFFECTIVE PRESIDENTS ($N = 265$)		ALL PRESIDENTS ($N = 504$)	
	Number Graduated	%	Number Graduated	%
University of Michigan	23	8.7	44	8.7
Yale University	14	5.3	15	3.0
Columbia University	13	4.9	16	3.2
Vanderbilt University	9	3.4	11	2.2
University of Texas	8	3.0	17	3.4
Stanford University	8	3.0	10	2.0
Harvard University	7	2.6	**	
Michigan State University	7	2.6	19	3.8
University of Wisconsin	7	2.6	10	2.0
Northwestern University	6	2.3	**	
University of Chicago	6	2.3	11	2.2
Ohio State University	5	1.9	11	2.2
Cornell University	5	1.9	**	
Florida State University	5	1.9	**	
University of North Carolina	5	1.9	10	2.0
University of South Carolina	5	1.9	12	2.4
University of Massachusetts	*		10	2.0
Total	133	50.2	196	39.1

*$n < 5$
**$n < 10$

trained slightly more than 50% of the effective presidents who responded to this survey question.

Considering all of the presidents who answered this question, over one-third of the respondents identify 13 colleges and universities. Once again, as Table 3.1 demonstrates, the University of Michigan is mentioned most frequently.

Doctoral institutions listed by both the effective presidents and the total group differ from those noted by Barr (1981) and Ferrari (1970). Of the 16 institutions included by Ferrari (1970), effective presidents list 8, and the total group of presidents mentions only 6. Barr's (1981) list of 21 universities granting the most doctoral degrees to presidents is more in keeping with our findings, with 12 noted by effective presidents and 9 reported by the total group.

The institutions training the most effective presidents at the doctoral level also tend to be headed by highly effective CEOs. For instance, of the 16 institutions listed, 12, or 75%, of them are under the leadership of people considered to be among the most highly acclaimed presidents in the country, that is, those nominated three or more times by their associates and qualified observers. In addition, when reputational rankings of doctoral programs in higher education are considered, 5 of the 16 institutions attended by effective presidents (Columbia University, Michigan State University, Stanford University, the University of Michigan, and the University of Texas) are included repeatedly in the listings of the top 10 institutions in the country (Johnson & Drewry, 1982; Keim, 1983).

Master's

Effective college presidents earned master's degrees from 106 different institutions. Once again, these presidents name the University of Michigan most often. As noted in Table 3.2, approximately 43% of the effective presidents received master's degrees from 1 of 12 different universities. In the total population of presidents responding to this question, 7 universities are listed by 10 or more people as the institution granting their master's degree.

Once again, it is clear that extremely effective presidents head the institutions preparing the largest number of effective presi-

Table 3.2

INSTITUTIONS GRANTING MASTER'S DEGREES

INSTITUTION	EFFECTIVE PRESIDENTS ($N = 245$)		ALL PRESIDENTS ($N = 508$)	
	Number Graduated	%	Number Graduated	%
University of Michigan	24	9.8	39	7.7
Columbia University	14	5.7	20	3.9
University of Notre Dame	14	5.7	19	3.7
Yale University	11	4.5	13	2.6
Vanderbilt University	7	2.9	10	2.0
Harvard University	5	2.0	**	
University of Illinois	5	2.0	**	
Catholic University of America	5	2.0	**	
University of South Carolina	5	2.0	10	2.0
University of Alabama	5	2.0	**	
St. Louis University	5	2.0	**	
University of Kansas	5	2.0	**	
Michigan State University	*		10	2.0
Total	105	42.6	121	23.9

*$n < 5$
**$n < 10$

dents at the master's degree level. Of the 12 institutions involved in training effective presidents at the master's degree level, 8, or 67%, are also headed by presidents considered to be highly effective by their associates and qualified observers. Thus, perhaps effective presidential leadership influences the educational quality of the institution's graduate programs.

Baccalaureate

A relatively large number of institutions offer effective college presidents their first experience in academe. As documented in

Table 3.3, only eight universities can claim to have granted baccalaureate degrees to four or more effective presidents. Because these top eight institutions represent only 16% of the effective presidents who reported baccalaureate degrees, it is clear that effective presidents choose from a larger pool of institutions granting baccalaureate degrees than those offering master's and doctoral-level training.

As for the total group of presidents, 15 universities granted the baccalaureate degree to five or more college presidents. By far, the University of Michigan matriculates the most presidents at this level. Interestingly, only slightly more than 20% of the total group of presidents attended 1 of these 15 universities.

Once again, at the baccalaureate level, we verify the close connection between effective presidential leadership and renowned academic programs. As we review the list of the eight institutions from which 16% of the effective presidents received their undergraduate degrees, we note that the presidents of five, or 63%, of these institutions are on our list of the most frequently nominated CEOs in the United States.

After analyzing all of the information available about the institutions attended by our presidents, we note significant differences in the public and private attendance record between the effective and representative groups. At the doctoral level, effective presidents are more likely than representative presidents to have attended a private institution ($p < .0001$). Moreover, the effective group is less likely to have earned master's degrees from public institutions than their representative counterparts ($p < .02$).

When considering the specific institutions attended by effective presidents, we find that several colleges and universities are involved in their educational preparation. Because the institutions conferring degrees to effective presidents include a mix of both public and private institutions, we believe the effective chief executive officer's selection of an institution goes much deeper than the college's or university's source of funding or location. Apparently, the academic reputation and the quality of program offerings are the key variables in decisions to attend a particular institution.

Table 3.3
INSTITUTIONS GRANTING BACCALAUREATE DEGREES

INSTITUTION	EFFECTIVE PRESIDENTS ($N = 269$) Number Graduated	%	ALL PRESIDENTS ($N = 539$) Number Graduated	%
University of Michigan	10	3.7	22	4.1
Yale University	6	2.2	6	1.1
Wake Forest University	6	2.2	8	1.5
Harvard University	4	1.5	8	1.5
Princeton University	4	1.5	5	0.9
University of Tennessee	4	1.5	8	1.5
Vanderbilt University	4	1.5	6	1.1
Southwest Missouri State University	4	1.5	*	
Michigan State University	**		7	1.3
University of Connecticut	**		6	1.1
City University of New York	**		6	1.1
University of Notre Dame	**		6	1.1
University of Wisconsin	**		6	1.1
University of Southern Mississippi	**		5	0.9
University of California	**		5	0.9
North Carolina State University	**		5	0.9
Total	47	15.6	109	20.1

*$n < 5$
**$n < 4$

Four institutions (University of Michigan, Yale University, Harvard University, and Vanderbilt University) are identified at all three degree levels as being among the universities preparing a substantial number of effective presidents. Given the fact that the presidents of these institutions were among the most frequently nominated effective CEOs in the country, we maintain that there is a linkage between effective presidential leadership and the academic excellence of an institution.

Academic Majors

Many people believe that the choice of institution to attend and the major field of study influence a person's ability to succeed in a leadership position. In fact, many business executives and academicians maintain that a "liberal" rather than a "professional" education is an essential credential for anyone interested in assuming a leadership position. With this in mind, we decided to see if there were any differences between effective and representative presidents in their choice of an area of study.

Doctoral Degree Major

Compared to previous studies related to the presidency in general (Barr, 1981; Carbone, 1981; Duea, 1981; Ferrari, 1970), we found an unexpectedly large number of presidents who hold doctorates in education. Our research shows that 36% of the effective presidents list education, with three-fourths of those majors being educational administration or higher education administration. The social sciences are a distant second in popularity, with 19% of the effective presidents noting economics, geography, international relations, history, political science, or sociology as majors. Philosophy and religion account for 7% of the doctoral fields. These results are similar to the findings related to effective leaders presented by Pruitt (1974) and Gilley and colleagues (1986). In both studies, over 40% of the presidents report having earned graduate degrees in education. The representative presidents more closely approximate the results of previous studies, in that slightly over 43% of them majored in education at the doctoral level and less than 10% of them hold degrees in the social sciences.

Master's Degree Major

The fields of study at the master's degree level for effective college presidents are typically the same as those at the doctoral level. Once again, the forerunner is education, with the second most popular field being the social sciences: anthropology, economics, geography, international relations, history, political science, and sociology. Finally, letters and philosophy or religion are reported as a distant third and fourth. Overall, the profile for effective and representative presidents is basically the same.

Baccalaureate Degree Major

At the baccalaureate level, the picture changes in two ways. First, there is a difference between the two groups, with effective presidents choosing majors in business less often than representative presidents ($p < .001$). The social sciences are listed most frequently as the chosen major by effective presidents at this level, whereas the largest group of representative presidents list education as their baccalaureate field of study. In addition, over twice as many effective presidents hold degrees in the social sciences as in education.

When we looked at differences in academic majors at all degree levels, we concluded that there is no best field of study for those aspiring to the presidency. However, for effective presidents, the academic path typically begins in the social sciences (usually history, political science, or economics). On the other hand, representative presidents usually begin their academic endeavors in either education or the social sciences.

Career Path

Typically, people who aspire to the presidency of educational institutions want to know about the previous experiences of those currently occupying the office. An examination of such information allows presidential hopefuls to assess their own professional backgrounds, to identify gaps in experience, and to develop appropriate career plans. Of course, numerous studies identify career-ladder trends for presidents in general, but only Pruitt (1974) focuses on the career path of effective CEOs.

With these thoughts in mind, we asked effective and representative presidents to identify their first position in academe, their last position before the presidency, the length of time they had spent in each of these two positions, the functional areas in which they served, and the types of institutions employing them. Their responses indicate that the work experience of the effective presidents is similar to that of the representative CEOs in some areas, but quite different in others.

First Position in Academia

Almost 60% of the effective college presidents say they entered the academy as faculty members, as compared with slightly less than 55% of the representative sample. Only two other positions are mentioned by more than 15 presidents: director and dean. This finding is consistent with studies conducted by Barr (1981), Ferrari (1970), and Moore, Salimbene, Marlier, and Bragg (1983), in which the most common point of entry for future presidents is the faculty ranks.

Over one-fourth of the effective group began teaching in the social sciences, with 20 presidents reporting history as their major field. Letters, education, physical science, and philosophy or religion round out the remaining top five teaching disciplines.

It is difficult to generalize about the initial position held by the 97 effective presidents who began their careers in other functional areas, because only 67 people provided responses. Only one area, student affairs, is listed by more than 10 effective presidents, whereas two areas, student affairs and external affairs, are named by the representative group. The remainder of the presidents is scattered among more than 15 other nonteaching posts.

Effective and representative presidents, who most frequently begin their academic careers in a four-year private institution, spent a relatively short time in their first positions. For instance, 53% of the effective respondents and 49% of the representative group report holding their first position for one to three years.

Moreover, less than 7% of the effective and representative presidents responding to this survey held their entry positions for more than 10 years.

Last Position Prior to Presidency

By far, the most common stepping-stone immediately before assuming the presidency for the effective group is the position of vice president for academic affairs or provost. It is not surprising that the largest group of effective presidents engage in academic administrative affairs at this point in their careers. General administration and instruction represent the second and third areas of choice. The next most frequently mentioned title held immediately before the first presidential post is that of dean, followed by assistant-to-the- and director. Apparently the difficulty involved in moving from a faculty position to the presidency is significant, as shown by the fact that only nine effective presidents report holding a faculty post at the time of their selection as chief executive officer. Again, these descriptors apply to the representative sample, with only the slight variation of director replacing assistant-to-the- as the third most frequently mentioned position.

Tenure in Position Immediately Prior to Presidency

Effective presidents spend approximately the same length of time in their last position before the presidency as they do in their first academic post, with 43% reporting less than 4 years. On the other hand, we note that almost 49% of the representative presidents remained in their positions prior to the presidency for 4 to 10 years. In addition, we find that effective presidents are less likely than representative presidents to work at a 2-year private institution immediately before their first presidency ($p < .004$).

Age When Selected for First Presidency

Most researchers have found that presidents typically assume their first chief executive officer's position when they are in their mid-40s (Bolman, 1965; Cohen & March, 1986; Gilley et al., 1986; McDonagh et al., 1970). Our results show that the greatest number of effective and representative presidents enter the office during their 40s. However, they tend to assume their first presidency earlier than reported by other researchers, with the mean being around 42 years of age. In addition, we find that representative presidents are more likely than effective presidents to assume the office after reaching 50 years of age ($p < .05$).

General Professional Experience

The vast majority of presidents participating in this study has worked in higher education administration for more than 15 years. But, in the experience arena, a major difference surfaced, in that, on average, representative presidents have fewer years of experience outside of higher education than their effective counterparts ($p < .0001$).

Upon reflection, we find that effective and representative presidents do not differ dramatically in terms of the career path they follow to the presidency. Apparently, all presidents recognize that their selection and credibility are dramatically influenced by faculty experience coupled with service as a provost or vice president for academic affairs. Therefore, they enter the academy as a faculty member, serve for a relatively short time in an instructional position, administer an academic affairs division briefly, and then become president of an institution.

The major difference between effective and representative presidents resides in the diversity of experience they bring to the presidency. For example, our effective presidents are not solely academically oriented in their professional backgrounds. As we noted earlier, representative presidents tend to have worked fewer years outside of higher education than those in the effective sample. Thus, because of their diverse experiences, effective presidents bring valuable information about managing other types of organizations to the higher education world.

CURRENT POSITION AND ACTIVITIES

When thinking about the present status of effective presidents, several questions come to mind. How many years have they been in their current presidency? Where are they serving? Are their campuses small or large? What kinds of salaries are they claiming? Do they participate in scholarly activities? For the first time we have answers to these questions.

We find that representative presidents have spent fewer years in their current presidency than those in the effective group ($p <$ .0001). Almost 75% of our effective chief executive officers spent five or more years in their present position, as compared with only 55% of the representative sample. In addition, almost one-third of the effective group has served in the current presidency for more than 10 years, whereas less than one-fourth of the representative group can claim the same length of service. Incidentally, the results of previous studies focusing on 2-year college presidents (which made no allowance for effectiveness) parallel our findings for the representative sample (Gilli, 1976; Vaughan, 1986). In terms of total years in the presidency, there are no differences between effective and representative presidents.

The discrepancy between head counts of institutions led by effective and representative presidents is significant ($p <$ .0001), with effective presidents more likely than the representative group to lead institutions with head counts of 20,001–30,000. In fact, average head counts are approximately 11,200 for the effective group and 5,200 for representative presidents. We also find that effective presidents are less likely than their representative counterparts to work at 2-year, private institutions ($p <$ .0001).

Even though both groups of presidents seem to be financially secure, it definitely pays to be viewed as effective. Exclusive of perquisites, representative presidents report an average annual salary of slightly more than $66,000, whereas effective presidents say they earn approximately $80,000 per year. Our findings show a difference in the earning power of the two groups, with effective presidents less likely than representative presidents to be in the lower income brackets ($p <$ .0001).

Past and present scholarly activity also seems to set the two groups apart. On average, effective CEOs have published significantly more books ($p <$ .001) and articles in refereed journals ($p <$ .005) than representative presidents. The difference between the two groups is notable when you consider published articles. Members of the effective group report an average of 12, whereas those in the representative sample average only 8 articles.

Membership in professional organizations is part of the scholarly activity of both effective and representative presidents. However, we find differences between the groups in two separate areas. Effective presidents are members of more professional organizations than representative presidents ($p < .03$). We also note that effective and representative presidents do not belong to the same organizations. The effective group names the American Council on Education and other national organizations with an emphasis on higher education more frequently than the representative group ($p < .001$ and $p < .006$, respectively). Furthermore, their involvement does not stop with paying dues and attending conferences. For instance, our results show than 63% of the effective presidents, as compared with 39% of the representative group, have provided service to a professional organization.

Thus, we find that, on average, effective presidents have spent more years in their current presidency, lead institutions with larger head counts, command higher annual salaries, publish more articles and books, and belong to more professional organizations than representative presidents. We believe their leadership effectiveness enables them to remain in their positions longer and, consequently, to be rewarded appropriately by their boards of trustees. Moreover, we believe their continued contributions to the academy through the publication of articles and their involvement in major national organizations signal that their effectiveness is recognized by colleagues.

PERSONAL TRAITS

People, in general, are usually fascinated by information about the personal characteristics of people who hold or have held a particular position. There have been numerous profiles of administrators in higher education (college presidents, vice presidents, and deans), governmental officials, and business executives, to name just a few. However, these profiles usually focus on the population in general rather than on people considered to be extremely successful in performing their duties.

In Pruitt's 1974 exploration of the personal backgrounds of

25 effective college presidents, he found some dramatic differences between the characteristics of his sample population and the previously reported traits of presidential incumbents. We were intrigued with the notion that there might be identifiable personal differences, so we asked the people involved in our study to provide relatively in-depth information about themselves. Upon analysis of our data, we conclude that there are, indeed, definitive differences between the personal attributes of effective and representative presidents. As we describe our findings, we will also compare and contrast our results with those from earlier studies on the college presidency.

Age

Age is one of the mysteries of life that evokes a particular kind of curiosity. Perhaps it is because we all have a sense that time is wasting and are afraid of failing to reach self-imposed goals. Or perhaps it is part of our inquisitive nature to wonder whether we measure up to others or have achieved what others have achieved in the same amount of time. We were curious about the age of effective college presidents. How long did it take them to reach such an exalted position, to be admired and respected by their colleagues?

Our study shows a difference in the ages of effective and representative presidents, with the representative group being younger ($p < .0001$). When comparing age ranges, we find the greatest number of effective presidents clustered between the ages of 50 and 59, whereas most members of the representative group are under the age of 50. Our findings about the effective group are in line with the results of other studies related to the presidency (Cohen & March, 1986; Ferrari, 1970; Gilley et al., 1986). However, we detect differences when we look at previously reported age ranges. For example, Cohen and March (1986) reported that 12% of all college presidents are under the age of 40 or over the age of 70 at any given time. Of the effective presidents who participated in our study, only 2% fit this classification.

Differences in age ranges become most apparent when you compare previous data about 2-year college presidents with our current findings regarding effective presidents. Vaughan (1986) and Brooks and Avila (1974) found that over one-half of the 2-year college presidents they studied were 50 years of age or younger. Interestingly, less than one-fourth of our effective presidents fell into this age bracket. Moreover, when you compare 2-year college presidents who are 51–60 years of age with our effective presidents, these percentages are virtually reversed. That is, over 52% of those deemed effective are 51–60 years old, as opposed to 38% of the 2-year college presidents (Vaughan, 1986). Therefore, effective presidents, in general, are older than their 2-year college counterparts.

Investigations regarding the age of CEOs in the corporate sector yield interesting results in light of our findings. Hise and McDaniel (1985) say that the mean age of CEOs is 56 years, with 34% between 60 and 69. In contrast, only 17% of our effective group is between 60 and 69 years of age, leading us to suggest that effective presidents tend to be younger than executives in business and industry.

On the basis of our findings, it is safe to say that effective presidents are not, as Cicero termed it, in the play's last act. Rather, they are individuals who reach the presidential position at an early age and make significant contributions to higher education administration for a long time.

Educational Background of Parents

In keeping with the results of previous studies (Barr, 1981; Ferrari, 1970; Vaughan, 1986), most of the presidents involved in this study report having parents who did not complete high school. Surprisingly, however, 50% of our effective presidents have fathers who did not finish high school. Furthermore, less than 25% of the effective presidents report having fathers who completed a bachelor's, a master's, or a doctoral degree.

Effective presidents are more likely than the representative group to have mothers who did not attend high school ($p < .04$). We find that 30% of the mothers of effective presidents have less than a high school education, compared with only 20% of the representative presidents. In addition, the majority of effective presidents have both mothers and fathers who did not attend college and, thus, are first-generation college graduates.

Even though many effective presidents come from families with little formal education, apparently they were taught early to appreciate higher learning. Their parents' belief in the ability of higher education to foster a better life for their children than they had encountered might be one of the reasons that effective presidents are willing to sacrifice so much for the cause. They have direct evidence of the impact that postsecondary education can have on an individual. Therefore, they work endlessly to ensure that the opportunity to receive an education will always be available to other interested people.

Immediate Family Unit

As expected, our data indicate that most presidents are married. For instance, 82% of the effective presidents and 85% of the representative sample are married. Of those who are not married, 8% of the effective group and 9% of the representative presidents have remained single. And only a small percentage of both effective and representative presidents is divorced: 5% of the effective group and 3% of the representative population. We also find that the vast majority of presidents has been married only once (79% of the effective and 78% of the representative).

In looking at other studies, we note that the percentage of effective presidents who are married is lower than was found by Bolman (1965), Ostar (1983), and Vaughan (1986), but this is consistent with the findings of Barr (1981). Probably discrepancies are due to the inclusion of several Roman Catholic presidents in our effective group.

Contrary to the common belief that presidential spouses are primarily professional volunteers for the institution, we find that almost 60% of the spouses of effective and representative presidents works outside the home. Of this group, approximately 70% belongs to the professional ranks: physicians, attorneys, professors, nurses, teachers, and educational administrators, among others. These results are revealing when compared with those from a study conducted by Ostar (1983) in which she found that only 32% of presidential spouses works outside the home.

On average, the family unit of effective and representative presidents is comprised of three children between 23 and 30 years of age. Based on their own ages, it is not surprising that representative presidents have younger children than effective presidents ($p < .007$ and $p < .02$, respectively), except in the case of a third child. In this instance, effective presidents are more likely than the representative group to have a college-age child ($p < .03$).

Political Affiliation

Most of the effective presidents who claim a political affiliation name the Democratic party, with the Independent and Republican parties placing second and third. Representative presidents are most frequently aligned with the Democratic and Republican parties, whereas the Independent party surfaces as a distant third choice. In fact, effective presidents are more likely than those in the representative group to identify themselves as Independents ($p < .009$).

Other Common Characteristics

In keeping with previous studies (Barr, 1981; Bolman, 1965; Brooks & Avila, 1974; Duea, 1981; Ingraham, 1968; Pruitt, 1974), our effective and representative presidents are overwhelmingly male, Caucasian, and Protestant. They are also most frequently first-born children who were born and currently live in states associated with the North Central accreditation region. Thus, in terms of sex, race, religious preference, birth order, and current residence, there are no distinct differences between effective and representative CEOs.

CONCLUSIONS

This new information about the characteristics of effective college presidents provides us with food for thought about the impact of early personal and professional experiences on leadership effectiveness. The profile of their personal attributes, although similar in some ways to the overall population of presidents, is different in other very intriguing areas. We will highlight the differences now.

The educational backgrounds of effective and representative presi-

dents differ in three distinct ways. Effective college presidents are less likely than their representative counterparts to have earned their first degree in business and to have completed their master's degree work at a public institution. In addition, effective presidents are more likely than representative presidents to have received their doctorates from a private institution.

In terms of their current status, effective and representative presidents are also different. For example, when compared with representative presidents, effective chief executives are more likely to lead institutions with larger student enrollments and less likely to be in the lower income brackets. Effective presidents are also less likely to have worked in a 2-year private institution immediately before assuming the presidency or to lead this type of college now. Moreover, representative presidents have spent fewer years in their current presidency than members of the effective group and are older when they initially assume the CEO's position.

In terms of service to the profession, effective presidents are more active and visible than their representative counterparts. For instance, effective presidents tend to publish more books and articles and are members of national professional organizations more frequently than representative presidents. Effective presidents also belong to different types of organizations than do members of the representative group.

Representative presidents have fewer years of experience outside the higher education environment than effective presidents. Thus, effective presidents possess knowledge of administrative and faculty responsibilities as well as comparative data about the management of external organizations.

The political affiliations of effective and representative presidents are different. Specifically, effective presidents are more likely than the representative group to identify themselves as politically independent.

Effective presidents differ from their representative colleagues in terms of their own age and the age of their children. For example, representative presidents are younger than effective presidents, which probably contributes to the fact that representative presidents have younger children than members of the effective group. In addition, effective presidents are more likely than representative CEOs to have a college-age child.

Effective presidents are more likely than the representative group to have mothers who did not attend high school. As noted earlier, many of the effective college presidents' parents did not graduate from high school. Perhaps the fact that their parents, especially their mothers, encouraged these men and women to advance (in both social status and education) well beyond their own level could have established in effective presidents an all-consuming desire to see that education is available to others in similar situations.

The picture we have now painted of effective college presidents is one of striving, achieving, and succeeding. We believe they prepared themselves, both educationally and experientially, for the important job of leading America's institutions of higher education. Perhaps because of their early personal and professional experiences, they lead with a special style, a concept we will explore in the next chapter.

·4·

Our Study: Leadership Characteristics of Effective Presidents

A president's ability to provide effective, empowering leadership is *the* key element in an institution's success or failure. It is, therefore, ironic that the academic community has been either unwilling or unable to define what makes a president effective. Of course, personal opinions and educated hunches about effective leadership abound, and search committees use them to select the leaders of our institutions. But considering higher education's acknowledged need for bold leadership, this approach is increasingly questionable.

Our research shows that there are distinct differences between the leadership styles of effective and representative presidents. We also have empirical data on behaviors that contribute to effective leadership, which are now available to presidential search committees and boards. Equally important, there is an instrument, the Fisher/Tack Effective Leadership Inventory, that, after further refinement, governing boards, aspiring presidents, and others in higher education can use as they seek to identify people with effective leadership potential. We think the refined instrument can be a significant tool for the higher education community to use in measuring potential leadership effectiveness.

As we said in chapter 1, the research results are based on the responses of 312 persons considered by their peers and associates to be effective presidents compared with the responses of 303 representative presidents. We wanted to compare those designated as effective presidents with an equivalent number of presidents, who, although not necessarily ineffective, represented the other side of the coin. Thus, we removed the names of the 412 presidents who were nominated, identified the remaining 2,388 presidents in our pool of 2,800 selected institutions, and grouped the institutions by region and sector of higher education. Then we selected a proportionate random sample, considering the number and types of presidents included in the effective listing.

We used the Fisher/Tack Effective Leadership Inventory (appendix D) to collect the information. We developed the instrument, pilot tested it with a randomly selected group of 400 current college presidents, and revised it after factor analysis. Through factor analysis, we identified five factors or indices to use in analyzing data: (1) management and leadership style index; (2) human relations index; (3) social reference index; (4) confidence index; and (5) image index. (See appendices B and C for information about the instrument.)

To understand as much as possible about effectiveness in the college presidency, we analyzed our data in a number of ways. As you would expect, we compared the responses of the effective (312) and representative (303) presidents to see whether there were any overall differences. We also wanted to know whether any differences resulted from the number of times a person was nominated as an effective president. So we compared the responses of the presidents who were nominated once, twice, and three times or more with each other and with the representative group.

We also compared the survey responses of the presidents we interviewed with each of these groups of effective presidents and with the representative sample.

Those particularly interested in the technical aspects of the study should see appendix G for a description of the statistical tools and methodology used in analyzing the survey responses. In addition, as a way of providing full disclosure of data collected, we include as appendices the frequency of responses to the statements on the Fisher/Tack Effective Leadership Inventory (appendix I) and the results of the statistical tests completed (appendices J–N).

CHARACTERISTICS OF EFFECTIVE COLLEGE PRESIDENTS

Clearly, this research effort has produced some very intriguing results related to the leadership behaviors of effective presidents. For instance, when we analyzed our data by factor, we found a statistically significant difference between the responses of effective and representative presidents on the confidence index ($p <$ .03). Yet there were no differences in the pattern of responses to the other four factors included in the instrument.

After identifying this important finding, we decided to look within the five factors to see if there were differences by item in the responses of effective and representative presidents. As we reviewed the results of the item-by-item analysis, we found differences between the two groups' responses to statements within three of the five indices. Interestingly, we found no significant difference between the responses to specific statements in the human relations and image indices. Thus, we believe both effective and representative presidents recognize the importance of having good interpersonal skills and of maintaining an image appropriate to the office. However, when you consider issues related to management and leadership style, social relationships, and confidence, the commonalities quickly disappear. From our findings, we noted the following characteristics of effective presidents.

Management and Leadership Style

The leadership style of effective presidents does not coincide with the "norm" and flies in the face of previously accepted practice in higher education. Specifically, on eight items within the management and leadership style index, we found significant differences when we (1) compared the responses of effective presidents and their representative counterparts and (2) analyzed the responses of effective presidents on the basis of frequency of nomination. Here are our findings about the leadership behaviors and attitudes of effective college presidents.

They value the respect of others. Effective and representative presidents differ markedly when it comes to their perceptions about the impact that the respect of others has on a person's leadership prowess. We found that, in general, effective presidents believe more strongly than representative presidents "that the respect of those to be led is essential" ($p < .04$).

On the basis of this evidence, we conclude that the leadership behavior of effective presidents does not depend on superficial popularity, collegiality, or acceptance. Perhaps this is true because effective presidents recognize that respect from faculty and administrative staff makes leadership possible.

Environmental and experiential factors prevent the philosophy of leading based on respect rather than on popularity from gaining widespread acceptance on college campuses. Most faculty members and administrators believe that higher education's nature requires the leadership of equals, a concept based on notions of collegiality and familiarity. This theme echos throughout the educational process and becomes the overarching concern in selecting administrative personnel. So it takes a strong individual to break away from this traditional view of collegial leadership and assume leadership based on strength of conviction and character. We maintain that effective presidents do not let their previous experiences with collegiality cloud the importance of leading the institution. They understand, and even appreciate, the collegial atmosphere but recognize that the institution cannot achieve its mission unless the CEO makes hard decisions based on logic rather than concerns about campus politics.

They believe in the work ethic. Our study revealed that effective presidents generally "tend to work long hours" to a greater degree than representative presidents ($p < .006$).

This finding supports conclusions drawn previously by researchers and writers like Cohen and March (1986), Kotter (1982), McClelland and Burnham (1976), and Peters and Austin (1985). And the 18 preeminent leaders we interviewed confirmed that effective presidents give their time and energy unselfishly to pursuing a dream. Naturally, we will have more to say about this idea in chapter 5.

Because of the all-encompassing nature of their position, effective presidents must be reminded frequently of the need to maintain balance in their personal and professional lives. Of course, the way presidents manage their time differs, but there must be balance if the CEO is to appear mentally and physically alert.

They take risks. As we analyzed our data, we noted that the more frequently nominated presidents have a stronger belief "that the effective leader takes risks." For instance, presidents nominated two or more times believe that effective leaders take more risks than do presidents who were nominated only once ($p < .04$).

As noted earlier, numerous authors and researchers maintain that a risk-taking mentality and an adventurous spirit are essential to effective leadership. As Gilley et al. (1986) indicate, effective presidents frequently "open the door 'before the knock is heard'" (p.14), and Peck (1983) says that effective presidents rely on intuitive judgment, as well as facts, in making decisions. They do not take unnecessary risks or act with reckless abandon. But once they have determined that the benefit outweighs the cost, they act quickly and decisively. As discussed in chapter 5, our 18 interviewees reinforce the fact that effective presidents take calculated risks, risks that almost always yield significant, long-term dividends for their institutions.

They don't rely on consensus. Is consensus taking essential to effective leadership? Our research findings indicate it is not. For instance, when we considered responses to the statement "Try to achieve consensus," we found that interviewed presidents believe less in the importance of achieving consensus than all other effective presidents ($p < .02$). This finding also sheds further light on their attitudes toward collegiality.

We believe effective leaders do not rely on or hide behind the prevailing view of their constituents in making decisions. Of course, effective presidents seek input and carefully consider the feelings of the majority about issues. Indeed, they seem to sense intuitively what the consensus is without polling. The effective president always seems to be ahead of the community, but not too far. However, presidential effectiveness is based more on making good decisions than on making decisions endorsed by most constituents.

Perhaps the difference in being an effective president and just being a president depends on making bold decisions, taking risks, and sometimes moving against the prevailing winds. In combination with these behaviors, the willingness to move ahead, either with or without consensus, is another characteristic of effective chief executive officers.

They support merit pay. We found that the most universally acclaimed presidents "believe in merit pay" more strongly than their colleagues who were nominated only once or twice ($p < .03$). Interestingly enough, Weiss (1984) notes that Japanese managers base compensation on performance rather than on seniority. He suggests that it is the merit-pay notion, rather than other issues such as involvement in decision making, that most dramatically influences the success of Japanese businesses. Perhaps we can learn something from the Japanese and from our effective presidents who recognize that you should not reinforce mediocrity and that you should reward different levels of performance and productivity. To do or think otherwise negatively influences the president's ability to lead and to be effective.

The controversy over merit pay is interesting and somewhat ironic. We have known for decades that people are not primarily motivated to work harder or to achieve greatness because of monetary rewards. Rather, they thrive on such things as recognition, the potential for advancement, and the job itself. Even with this information in hand, many presidents still want to structure elaborate systems that are divisive and expensive and do not produce the desired results. Although effective presidents support merit pay, they are not prone to develop processes that constrict their institutions' ability to reward productivity. They keep things simple and responsive.

They support creative dissonance. Effective presidents thrive on diversity and encourage creativity. We base this conclusion on the fact that the interviewed presidents say they "encourage creative types even though often in disagreement" to a greater extent than all of the other effective presidents ($p < .05$).

Perhaps this situation exists because effective presidents have a high tolerance for dealing with individualists. They champion people who have different ideas, question everything, comply with little, and do not speak, look, or behave like everyone else. As our 18 effective presidents say, creative individuals not only dream strange dreams, but they also have the capacity to make their dreams come true. In keeping with the idea of creative dissonance, effective presidents tend to select staff members who have the courage and stamina to be themselves and voice their opinions, even when their ideas will not be popular.

They support organizational flexibility. It is not surprising that representative presidents "believe in organizational structure" more strongly than effective presidents ($p < .05$). In many instances, representative presidents allow organizational charts, policies, and procedures to deter them from making the "right" decision for their institutions. We also have to assume that representative presidents frequently use the formal organizational structure as a crutch to justify decisions or to delay the inevitable.

Although recognizing that any organization must have structure and a chain of command, effective chief executives believe in organizational flexibility, especially in terms of communicating within the institution. As Gilley and colleagues (1986) point out, college presidents who are considered successful do not recognize organizational boundaries but go straight to the heart of the problem, even if this means dealing with someone four levels removed from the presidential position. In describing Frank Borman, head of Eastern Airlines, a staff member says, "If he is presented with a problem, he is likely to go to the person who knows about the problem, ignoring normal channels" (Hill, 1984, p. 27). So we conclude that effective presidents recognize and use the organizational structure to their advantage but don't allow it to impede their work. They solve problems by seeking out accurate, reliable information wherever and whenever they can find it.

They don't speak spontaneously. Representative presidents report that they speak spontaneously to a greater degree than effective presidents ($p < .0001$). In addition, the more frequently a president was nominated, the less likely he or she was to speak spontaneously ($p < .01$, when those who were nominated once were compared with presidents nominated two or more times).

What does this finding mean? From our vantage point, it means that representative presidents continue to act in ways that reinforce collegiality and openness in academe. They don't realize that the role of the president is different. Perhaps because of previous training and professional experiences, some presidents have been conditioned to believe in brainstorming with peers and colleagues and in sharing everything they know with constituent groups. In contrast, our findings, as well as those of Bennis and Nanus (1985) and J. W. Gardner (1986a), support the idea that effective presidents think before they speak. Effective presidents might *appear* to speak spontaneously, but they have definitely thought about the content and delivery before beginning to talk. To the extent possible, they plan every communication carefully, to the point of scripting comments, as well as speeches.

Effective presidents recognize that they must act and speak responsibly and think through the complexities of an issue before making statements. Such action promotes continuity, reliability, and predictability, elements that engender trust and respect in leaders. Because of his or her position, no president should make remarks lightly. It is off-the-cuff or satirical comments that undermine the ability to provide steadfast, effective leadership.

Social Reference

The results of our research effort show that certain socially oriented factors influence presidential effectiveness, and those who lead higher education institutions must consider them carefully. When compared with representative presidents and each other, we found that the most highly effective presidents have a different philosophy about the social aspects of their position. They are less concerned about being liked and believe less in close collegial relationships. They are also more concerned about the substance of their leadership than such peripheral issues as dress.

Being liked is a nonissue. Consider the statement in our inventory that reads, "As a college president, I am primarily concerned about being liked." When we analyzed the responses of effective and representative presidents, we found that effective presidents are less concerned about being liked than are their representative counterparts ($p < .01$).

These results lead us to believe that effective presidents are more concerned about their impact on the institution and the achievement of a dream than about being liked by their colleagues. In other words, they are more interested in results and respect than in popularity. Effective presidents recognize that no decision pleases everyone and that decisive leaders cannot compromise their principles, values, or leadership potential to maintain the favor of individuals or groups. They make decisions that benefit the organization and the majority. They call the shots as they see them (which usually hit the bull's eye) and, consequently, lead from a position of strength and respect.

Collegial relationships are not a top priority. Effective presidents definitely "believe in close collegial relationships" less than their representative counterparts ($p < .008$). In addition, the more frequently a president was nominated, the more likely she or he was to maintain this position. In other words, presidents who were nominated two or more times report that they believe less in close collegial relationships than do persons nominated only once ($p < .04$).

In his early work on bureaucracy, Weber concludes that collegiality hinders leadership and that overemphasis on collegial relationships slows the operation of the organization (Gerth & Mills, 1946). In higher education, we emphasize collegiality in our actions and training programs. Then we wonder why leadership is difficult. So leadership and collegiality are, on the surface, antithetical. Effective presidents cannot be close friends with members of the campus community if they expect to exercise leadership and maintain objectivity about the enterprise. Although they support close collegial relationships among faculty, as presidents they are not part of the collegial fabric.

Representative presidents might disavow the notion of maintaining significant distance from colleagues, particularly faculty, because they believe in the concept of collegial governance. Attitudes about leadership are indeed formed on the basis of experience. Many presidents began their professional careers as faculty members and then moved into administration. Perhaps in the process of gaining academic experience, some were brainwashed into believing that familiarity and openness with colleagues create a utopian environment. Many less confident people attempt to establish close personal relationships in all settings. They mistakenly believe that close relationships will help them achieve their goals in the organization.

It is our position that maintaining social and psychological distance contributes to effective leadership. But this distance is not uniformly distributed, and we will expand on this point in chapter 5. As the 18 presidents we interviewed say, most of the people they work with do not view them as colleagues. However, they do maintain a strong relationship with their closest associates, defined typically as selected members of their executive cabinet. So, although most people on campus certainly don't know them, they do, on a selective basis, have close relationships to help them achieve their goals.

A dress-for-success attitude is missing. As we reviewed our research results, another interesting finding emerged: Representative presidents report more often that they "dress well" than do effective presidents ($p < .05$). Although we are certain that effective presidents are conscious of the need to look good, they apparently are not overly concerned about their wardrobes. Perhaps this is true because effective presidents have more to worry about than whether or not they are wearing the right clothes. They do, in fact, give more attention to the substance of the presidency—where the institution is headed and what they can do to enhance success on the part of faculty and staff within the institution.

McClelland and Burnham's (1976) findings support our research results showing that better managers are more concerned about the institution than about their own personal prestige. On the other hand, effective presidents must make sure that other people view them as powerful, and appearances help. As

Kotter (1977) notes, successful managers "sometimes carefully select, decorate, and arrange their offices in ways that give signs of power" (p. 123). Again, because effective presidents must manage their images, they need to "look the part," which includes dressing appropriately. However, they are apparently not as concerned about the cut of the particular suit they are wearing as they are about what they have to say and how others view the presidency.

Indications of Confidence

We found that the way presidents conduct their business (or the aura they project) contributes to their ability or inability to be effective. Specifically, when we looked at responses to the three items in the confidence index, a difference emerged ($p < .03$) between effective and representative presidents. We find that effective presidents scored higher on the confidence index (as defined by the items included in this index) than their representative counterparts. Interestingly, there was no significant difference in the responses to one of the three items, namely, "am rarely in keeping with the status quo." However, we see that representative presidents "believe in the institution at all costs" to a greater degree than effective presidents ($p < .005$) and that interviewed presidents do not appear to make decisions as easily as all of the other effective presidents ($p < .03$).

This evidence leads us to conclude that effective presidents see themselves and their institutions differently than do representative CEOs. Therefore, another trait of effective presidents has emerged: confidence in their leadership ability, which is fed by their commitment to higher education in general rather than to one institution in particular. Here is more information about this particular trait of effective college presidents.

They believe in the institution as a facilitator of dreams. What rationale exists to explain why representative presidents "believe in the institution at all costs" to a greater degree than do effective presidents ($p < .005$)? Moreover, the more frequently a person was nominated, the less likely he or she was to agree with this statement ($p < .04$). This dichotomy exists perhaps because effective presidents are more concerned with the mission of the institution (and their dream or vision for it) than with the institution itself. Although effective presidents see the institution as a structure through which to accomplish social good, representative presidents might see it as an end in itself and consider only what is "best" for the individual campus.

We also believe effective presidents do not see their institutions as living, breathing entities. The institution, as viewed by effective presidents, must contribute to both the overall purpose of higher education and improved living conditions for citizens throughout the world. Sometimes, because effective presidents can see the "big picture," they make decisions that others might view as not being in the best interest of the institution. However, in the long run, both the institution and society usually benefit from the effective president's action. As indicated in chapter 5, our interviews confirm the fact that effective presidents sacrifice immediate gains and even short-term institutional recognition for long-term societal improvement.

Decision making does not appear to be so easy. We find that the interviewed presidents do not appear to make decisions as easily as all of the other presidents ($p < .03$). Naturally, the interviewed presidents realize they must make the hard decisions, but they do not want to give the impression that the process or the result was quick or not seriously contemplated. These interviewed presidents might anguish, and even hurt, while making a decision, and they want those who are affected by the decision to know that the process was difficult, in order to lend credibility to their actions. They know that the presidential position is on the line with every decision. Overall, if presidents don't put their jobs on the line from time to time, they might not be taking enough risks.

Effective presidents don't hesitate to make decisions. They don't create a committee to spread the responsibility around or delay the decision. If they create a committee, its objective is to secure responses from the people involved. Interestingly, however, although effective presidents worry about securing adequate feedback, they are more than willing to make decisions that go against the wishes of their constituent groups but that, in their view, benefit the institution.

HOW EFFECTIVE PRESIDENTS ARE DIFFERENT

As we compared the perceived leadership behaviors and attitudes of effective and representative presidents, we were intrigued by the number of differences we found. In contrast with their representative counterparts, effective presidents are strong leaders who believe less in close collegial relationships, work long hours, are less concerned about being liked, and rely more on respect than popularity as a leadership principle. They also speak only after thinking about the subject at hand and are more concerned about the substance of their leadership than about outward symbols of success, such as dress. Another hallmark of effectiveness in the presidency is the belief in the purpose of higher education rather than "the institution at all costs." In addition, they believe in organizational flexibility more strongly than representative presidents and, therefore, might be able to move the institution along more readily toward accomplishing a dream or a vision.

Effective presidents who were nominated multiple times are not overly concerned about achieving consensus and are unafraid to take a stand on controversial issues such as support for the concept of merit pay. In addition, they take evaluated risks, do not appear to make decisions flippantly or too easily, and encourage creativity, actions typically associated with self-confidence.

As we mentioned in the early part of this chapter, we were just as interested in what we found as what we didn't find in analyzing our results. For instance, we found no statistically significant differences between the responses of representative and effective presidents to the statements about human relations and image. Therefore, we maintain that all presidents value effective human relations and recognize the importance of being able to communicate effectively with their constituents. This conclusion is reasonable in that higher education is a people-oriented enterprise and individuals who achieve positions of leadership must exemplify concern for the welfare of others and be trustworthy and loyal to their constituents.

We also conclude that all presidents have an image to uphold and that most of them do so with great finesse. Unquestionably, when a person moves into the presidential suite, a particular image of leadership is bestowed on her or him. However, effective presidents capitalize on their finely honed human relations skills and the inherited presidential image because of their unique leadership qualities, their different attitudes about social interactions, and their more than adequate level of confidence.

·5·

What Some of America's Best Presidents Say about Leadership

To this point, we have been concerned with the results of formal surveys and measurable differences between presidents considered effective and those representing the whole. Granted, such differences are important. However, we wanted to understand more about the intricacies of presidential effectiveness.

Consequently, 18 people were interviewed who, on the basis of frequency of nomination within the four sectors of higher education, are considered to be among America's most effective chief executive officers. We wanted to know the differences and similarities of presidents representing 2-year, 4-year, public, and private institutions. Moreover, we felt that using such a broad-based group might prevent the research results from being viewed as one-sided or based on a popularity contest. Incidentally, if we had used plurality as the only criterion for including presidents in the interview process, those at 4-year private institutions would have dominated the list.

Initially, we planned to interview 20 presidents, or 5 from each sector, but were unable to do so because of the limited number of 2-year private institutions. Apparently, the small number contributed to the nomination of only three institutional officers from that type of institution. Because of the need to maintain somewhat equal representation in the interview process, each of these presidents was interviewed. Therefore, the number of presidents interviewed was 18 instead of 20. As we mentioned in chapter 1, 3 presidents in the 4-year private sector opted not to participate in the campus-based interviews, so, ultimately, 21 presidents were contacted in the process of finalizing the list of the 18 presidents to be involved.

We chose to use the guided interview as our research tool because it is considered to be an appropriate means of gathering in-depth information from individuals. Given the fact that these presidents have risen to the top of the administrative hierarchy in higher education, we felt that they would not be shy, retiring types and that they would have a firm grasp of their strengths and weaknesses. Therefore, a set of questions was developed, pilot tested, refined, and posed to these 18 highly regarded presidents (appendix G).

Because this book is designed to help eliminate some of the mystery surrounding presidential effectiveness, we have chosen to focus primarily on the questions related to what the 18 presidents thought made them effective leaders. As you will see, we have taken the liberty of talking about these presidents as a group. Granted, no one person can possess all of the traits described, for no one is superhuman. However, on the basis of our interview data, we feel comfortable in profiling them as a group because their philosophies of leadership and leadership behaviors reflect tremendous commonality.

PERSONAL VALUES

Most people assume that all great leaders have a strong set of values and beliefs that guide their actions. Thus, as we conducted our interviews, we looked for clues to the personal philosophies held by these 18 presidents. As we analyzed the transcripts of the 2-hour sessions, we identified three primary principles that these outstanding individuals seem to have internalized. They are an unfaltering belief in the value of higher education coupled with a personal desire to make a difference in the scheme of things, genuine respect for others, and faith in their own and their associates' ability to accomplish the tasks at hand.

They are completely committed to what they do. During the interviews with our 18 presidents, the strongest common trait that surfaced was an intense and deep-seated belief in what they are doing. They place great value on education in general and higher education in particular, because they view the educational experience as a way of helping others improve themselves. The words of one interviewed president seem to capture the essence of this commitment:

> I really believe in American higher education, and I am sure it's the ultimate security and economic system for our country. I have that faith within me, and I think I'm more effective because I'm not just promoting something or working for something in which I don't believe.

Because of their futuristic view, these presidents spend much time and concentration on holistic thinking, which leads to integrating their work with societal interests. There is a definite vision that surfaces with all these presidents, a vision for the institution and for all of higher education that causes them (and everyone around them) to stretch to meet the mark. They are never satisfied but are always striving, always thinking, always considering ways to improve the quality of life for people throughout the globe. They think great thoughts that often lead to the creative solution of problems or to an improved condition for their constituents.

Interestingly, when discussing their work, these effective leaders exude enthusiasm. It is exciting for them to be part of higher education in this country, to work with others on its behalf, and to be a catalyst for positive change. They also feel fortunate to have the opportunity to bring forth new ideas and help shape the future.

For these select few, the presidency is not simply a job or position; it is a calling. There is a sense of moral obligation, even servitude, that gives rise to the feeling that they are making an important contribution to society. Respect for the office is apparent but not the type that leads to stagnation. Rather, it is a respect that evolves from doing something they love. The position they hold represents more than a vocational choice; it is also their hobby, their recreation, and their being. Thus, their dedication to this calling is invigorating and fulfilling, in and of itself.

They genuinely respect others. Unquestionably, these presidents emphasize the worth of others. To them, everyone in the organization holds a special place of importance, whether senior faculty members, maintenance engineers, board members, or clerical workers. Moreover, they recognize that nothing can be accomplished if individuals in the organization suffer. And they know that even the most grandiose plans can be achieved if individual worth is underscored and valued.

When dealing with others, the interviewees exhibit innate fairness, unquestionable integrity, and honesty in personal and professional relationships. They handle people-related issues in a straightforward manner so everyone knows where they stand. As the president of a private university says, "Don't drive such a hard bargain that you leave people bitter and unhappy."

These presidents are concerned about the personal and professional growth of colleagues and exhibit their concern by using a certain humanness when engaged in problem solving. They seem to have the uncanny knack of knowing how people will react in given situations, and they use this perceptive power to their advantage. Consequently, the welfare of others (faculty, students, administrative staff, and so on) is a significant consideration for them when they make or translate decisions relating to the institution.

They are true leaders in that the reactions of others do not dictate their decisions. As one president notes, "It is more important to be respected for doing the job than it is to be popular." Even so, these effective presidents are aware of how organizational policies affect individuals. When others hurt, they also feel the pain. However, because they know the importance of making good decisions, they often have to put their personal feelings on hold as they advance the cause of higher education. For example, after underscoring his strong belief in the people with whom he works and the value of their ideas, the president of a 2-year, private college says, "If I have to be an autocrat sometimes and if I have to come down hard, I have the ability to do it."

They believe in themselves and others. These 18 effective presidents admit to having high standards for others, combined with confidence that their colleagues will rise to the occasion. According to one president, "I have high expectations, not only for myself but for the people who work with me."

There is an almost Herculean belief in the strength of self, causing them consistently to exude confidence and believe in their ability to accomplish what they set out to do. Consider the words of a 4-year public university president: "I just don't believe in surrender. I don't believe in ever giving up on anything. I don't think there's any substitute for victory." Added reinforcement for this point comes from another president:

> Obviously you don't win all of the battles, but I certainly don't view, as some have said, that when you look back if you've won 51% of them you've been successful. I think you should get a piece of everything you have ever tried.

This strong sense of self does not develop overnight. It evolves over years of struggle and determination. Because of their strong self-confidence, these presidents feel free to be themselves. As the president of a 4-year private institution notes, "I'm often seen as a high risk, impulsive, impatient . . . gutsy person— I don't scare." Thus, effective presidents don't change to please others. Instead, they follow their own consciences.

According to this group, their effectiveness is often a result of surrounding themselves with good people. They definitely realize that the job cannot be done alone. According to one president, effective CEOs "have to hire the very best people they can find, even if they are older, even if they are brighter, and even if they are more experienced."

They also reward their staff members for having the courage and stamina to be themselves and to voice their convictions. In other words, effective presidents do not reward yes-people but nurture individuals who have different ideas and are not afraid to speak up. In fact, these effective presidents do not consider the trait of loyalty to be as important as intelligence, good judgment, and good human relations skills. At least they did not say so.

Finally, because they are professionally secure in what they want to achieve, these presidents allow a great deal of freedom in problem solving and decision making. They give their staff members room to experiment. They provide encouragement and even informally insist that others think differently. They also allow others to make a marginal number of mistakes. Yet, when others experience success, they are generous with the credit. As the president of a private 2-year college puts it, "you have to be a person who is willing to share all of the successes and to take all of the blame."

ABILITY AND SKILLS

It goes without saying that this group of presidents is intelligent and astute. They are quick studies and possess the ability to think fast on their feet. Because of their understanding of educational issues and their ability to identify trends, they have unlimited ideas about how to improve higher education at the national, state, and local levels. Moreover, there is a deep understanding of their respective institutions: how the institutions contribute to the whole, where they are going, and why they are moving in a particular direction.

To achieve their goals, these 18 presidents do not take things personally. Issues are intellectual and are dealt with on that basis rather than on a personal level. According to the CEO of a major midwestern university:

> It never occurs to me to take personally an issue with which someone disagrees. I always believe the discussions are based on intellectual issues, even if they aren't. As a result, I don't waste time, effort, and emotional energy wondering why it is that Dr. Y doesn't believe the way I do about something.

Finally, many members of this elite group attribute their success to unadulterated luck, or being in the right place at the right time. However, from talking with them, we conclude that their luck has been contrived, based on their intuitive ability to analyze, to size up situations, and to recognize opportunities and seize them. Because of their past experiences, both educational and professional, they have made sound decisions that have advanced their institutions and, subsequently, their careers. So perhaps it is not luck at all that has contributed to this group's effectiveness. Rather, it is a combination of their strong sense of self, a high degree of confidence in themselves and others, the value they place on individual worth, a willingness to take risks, and the courage to win.

LEADERSHIP STYLE

For decades we have wondered why some people can lead with such apparent ease and why it is almost impossible for others to move a group forward. With this nagging question in mind, we asked some of the best presidents in the nation to describe their leadership styles. As a result of our conversations, we identified certain beliefs and actions that can be considered prerequisites to leadership success. Interestingly, our interview data verify, in most cases, the research results described in chapter 4. Moreover, these 18 presidents have contributed substantially to our understanding of leadership by confirming that effective presidents exhibit certain generic behaviors. And, perhaps just as important, they have helped us explain why these behaviors are so critical to leadership success.

They are action oriented. The greatness of leaders is usually determined by actions rather than words. And, in many cases, the process of achieving goals becomes as important as the end result. When talking with these effective academic leaders about their leadership style, it became apparent that one key to accomplishing objectives is to take a proactive posture on a day-to-day basis. They do not wait for things to happen. Instead, they shape the future by creating, as well as capitalizing on, opportunities. According to the president of a public university, such a futuristic attitude is imperative: "I try to stay ahead of things. I wake up early in the morning thinking things over in my mind, trying to get answers to the problems."

When describing the way in which they deal with problems

and issues, the 18 presidents consistently use words such as *tenacious, determined, persistent,* and *impatient.* As one president puts it, "I'm a very impatient person. I expect to get things done yesterday because that's the way I work."

According to these 18 presidents, decisiveness and the willingness to stick to one's guns are two of the most important requirements for presidential success. As the CEO of a 2-year institution suggests, "When a decision is made and a direction established, I take it to people forcefully without wavering." We also note that the most effective presidents are able to convince others to accept decisions because these decisions are rarely made spontaneously and are based on the opinions of those to be affected by the proposed action.

They accept authority and responsibility in governance. Effective presidents decentralize the decision-making process to the extent that decisions are made at the lowest possible organizational level. As we said earlier, those considered most effective by their peers realize they cannot do everything. So these presidents give appropriate, but sometimes limited, decision-making authority. They encourage honest communication within the institution, for they seek advice and hear the things that others say. In this respect, there is an open organizational climate that encourages and promotes exchange of ideas from people at all levels of the institution.

However, all voices are not equal, and not all decision-making authority is shared. The more difficult or controversial the issue, the more autocratic these effective leaders tend to become. As one college president suggests:

> Most of the time I am democratic, in the sense of allowing lots of input but reserving the right to make the decision that I have to make. There are times when all the information might tell you to go in one direction, but in your heart you know you shouldn't. And so you don't.

Thus, they maintain the authority to call a spade a spade and tightly control some aspects of governance, aspects usually related to information flow, fund-raising efforts, and budgetary decisions.

Another important aspect of these presidents' leadership

styles is that they are open-minded and willing to reconsider official postures taken in the past. Naturally, they encourage their co-workers to do likewise. When necessary (and certainly not frequently), they reverse decisions and take action to correct situations that are not in the best interest of the institution. This creates a climate conducive to calculated risk taking and change. Security, rather than fear, motivates the actions of others, which, in turn, breeds loyalty to both the institution and its leaders. For the interviewees, true strength in leadership is the ability and willingness to press forward and take risks regardless of past events.

They have a penchant for work, work, and more work. Although they do not attend many committee meetings, these effective leaders admit to spending long, grueling hours preparing for a single meeting, especially when the stakes are high. We detected a certain pride when several presidents revealed that they are often among the best informed people present, even when the topic is far removed from the office of the president. According to one president:

> I'm always well prepared. In fact, in most meetings I'm the best prepared person present. That surprises most people who are meeting with me for the first time. I always have more questions in the meeting than anybody else. That's not because I'm smarter, and it's not because I know more in this area but because I come prepared.

This select group has a self-proclaimed high capacity for work and clearly expects the same of those who surround them. The president of a major university sums up the whole idea:

> I work hard and where I have been successful it's because I'm willing to get up earlier in the morning and stay up later at night than the average person. The fact of the matter is that the game will go to the person who'll work the hardest, and I work hard.

Not only do these presidents usually work more than 50 hours a week, but they also are able to accomplish more than the average person within that time. They attack their work in a fast and efficient manner, making us wonder how staff members maintain the energy level necessary to keep pace. But, because the presidency is such an integral part of their lives, the interviewees see little unusual about a person capable of consistently accomplishing 70 hours of work in 50 hours. As one CEO puts it, "I can work, and I work fast; I also can work really long hours, and it doesn't bother me."

They see the lighter side of things. Even though they spend most waking hours performing presidential duties, these effective presidents are still able to see the lighter side of life. The leadership of higher education institutions is serious business; yet, they do not take themselves too seriously. They recognize the necessity of levity when the negative aspects of situations seem to outweigh the positive. It is apparent that, for this group, a sense of humor takes the edge off anxiety-ridden circumstances and serves as a safety valve when tension runs high.

We conclude that the leadership style of our most effective presidents is best described as leading by example. They serve as both catalyst and facilitator for achieving goals and believe they can accomplish greatness by working with others in a sensitive, respecting manner. For this group, the achievement of a goal is not one-dimensional; rather, it results from the interaction of several factors including persistence, continuity, controlled governance, calculated risk taking, and loyalty.

HUMAN RELATIONS

During the interview process, we asked each president to describe his or her human relations skills. When answering this question, these presidents list characteristics that generally promote a positive organizational climate based on an upbeat attitude when dealing with others. The reason for this positive attitude is simple: They genuinely like people, and it shows.

They are warm, outgoing people. Typically, the most effective presidents are outgoing and attempt to get along well with everyone. Interpersonal contacts between the interviewees and those with whom they work most closely are candid and friendly. When there is social and psychological distance, it seems to occur naturally rather than in a contrived manner. However, even though members of this elite group attract people easily because of their friendly nature, it does not mean that they are loud and boisterous or attempt to be the life of the party. Indeed, their warmth and caring for others is balanced by a degree of reservation and temperance, because they recognize that a president cannot lead effectively by being a buddy with colleagues.

They maintain self-control. Effective presidents recognize the need to maintain the legitimacy of the office if they are to lead. The president is *always* the president, so there is a delicate balance between expressed affection and the image of strength he or she must exhibit. Hence, there are rarely extreme shifts in mood, at least none apparent to those outside of the executive's inner circle of colleagues and friends. It goes without saying that these presidents feel extreme moods, but rarely, if ever, do they let others see them. What people do see is stability derived from exhibited control, making people feel that they are in the presence of a mature person capable of making sound decisions. As one university president remarks, "I almost never get angry in public, and I don't tend to get euphoric in public either. I think that kind of consistency and confidence . . . is very important."

They use power with finesse. The most effective academic leaders' view of human relations becomes especially apparent in their discussion of power. There is no doubt that their governing boards grant them the authority to make decisions regarding appointments and budgetary matters. But, for this group, the issue of power is broader in scope. These presidents recognize that their power reaches beyond the official authority vested in them by the board of trustees. Actually, they believe that power relates to how others perceive them as leaders. Without the confidence and support of those served, the president is powerless. Presidents realize that power comes from respect earned when they are seen as fair, honest, and impartial on a personal level. Furthermore, by capitalizing on strong human relations skills and mutual respect, they maintain an atmosphere of trust, decency, and integrity.

The power possessed by the interviewees is not used to lord over subordinates or to manipulate others against their will. Rather, these presidents use power to influence and persuade in order to achieve goals. Effective presidents maintain credibility by using power sparingly and only when absolutely necessary. Although they realize they have the power to fire people or keep them dangling, these presidents do not enjoy playing power games. They are not high-handed power brokers who hold all the cards. Instead, they prefer to draw their strength from the willingness of others to become involved in and support their efforts. In fact, one private university president equates the use of legitimate power with dynamite when he says, "It should be well placed, used cautiously, and used very rarely."

In keeping with this philosophy, effective presidents do not typically govern by the use of outright power; they might have it, but they rarely use it. Rather, one president states:

> You lead men and women by inspiring and elevating them to think beyond their immediate horizons. . . . You exercise influence by showing people a vision of how they can be better. You empower them to think beyond their current status.

They are visible, but they share the credit. These presidents know that, to influence and persuade others, they must share the credit for successes. In fact, they are all too willing to give credit to others who deserve it. When they are in the limelight, they promote the institution and enhance its image. The publicity they receive is neither egocentric nor used for personal gain. Instead, effective presidents view it as something that should be done to improve the academic communities they serve. Because these presidents' closest associates know the way in which they handle visibility, there is little room for petty jealousies.

We conclude that, above all, the human relations skills of these effective presidents promote trust. Subordinates and members of governing boards alike ultimately believe in these leaders and trust that decisions are made and actions are taken for the good of the institution and not for personal gain. Effective presidents care about others, and they believe in helping people become all they can become. The most effective presidents create hope by encouraging others to achieve excellence regardless of the task.

PHILOSOPHICAL NATURE

Are the most effective academic leaders philosophical by nature? Are they visionaries or dreamers? We asked each of those interviewed these questions and concluded that our presidents are caught up in a dream and have a vision for their institutions. As a group, the interviewees are reflective. They think carefully about directions, consequences, and ultimate results of actions. They reach decisions by considering more than just short-range consequences; they consider secondary and tertiary results on a regular basis. By looking forward and seeing the way things can be, they make decisions in light of a larger vision.

When considering the broader scope, our 18 presidents attempt to integrate important societal issues with the educational enterprise and usually have a hand in developing national policy. They use information about trends, issues, problems, and opportunities when they chart a course for their institutions, solve problems, or create new opportunities.

They view the institution as a way to accomplish goals rather than as an end in itself. Thus, effective presidents change the institution to accomplish the vision. They take an idea, determine how to accomplish it, and move forward even if, in the short run, the decision is painful for the institution because, in the long term, it could benefit society and the institution.

The most effective presidents are dreamers firmly grounded in reality. They can look into the future and see a more desirable state of affairs for the institution, the state, the world, and the human condition. According to the president of a major eastern university, "If you don't think in terms of the future, you have no present. If you are not involved in the future, you are not involved in the present."

Perhaps the thing that sets these presidents apart from their peers is that they take the time to dream and that they base their aspirations on realism and the ability to achieve their goals. They are not pie-in-the-sky or idle dreamers. These leaders have been highly successful because they can integrate their dreams and visions into day-to-day business. They close the gap between dreaming and making things happen by translating their dreams into reality.

OBSTACLES

Our group of presidents identified many issues impinging on their professional effectiveness, but they mentioned funding most frequently by far. First and foremost, they realize that a lack of resources influences morale, making it difficult to accomplish the institution's mission. Under financial constraints, people sometimes cannot complete even the simplest tasks because they feel dissatisfied with their workplace and compensation. Also, when resources are scarce, presidents find themselves devoting an enormous amount of time to trying to maximize the value of the dollars received. This is time they could spend in more productive ways.

A second category of obstacles facing these presidents centers around bureaucracy. Sometimes creativity is lost when excessive paperwork becomes too restrictive and standardized. By the time plans are approved, many ideas have lost their spark and sense of urgency. Public sector presidents, who frequently must deal with voluminous policies and procedures, as well as increasing interference from government, point especially to the excesses of bureaucracy. Without question, federal and state agencies have tentacles that grow and grab a university or college, making it extremely difficult to lead. Just dealing with a bureaucracy demoralizes presidents and wastes their time.

Generally, time is critical for effective presidents. There is never enough of it. They accomplish tasks and meet deadlines, but frequently at the expense of sleep. Due to its limited nature, time affects these presidents' interactions with others. Effective presidents must put their appointments and requests in order of priority to avoid wasting time on undeserving issues. Hence, although accessible, the effective president's door is not always open.

The 18 leaders tell us that, although they generally appear to have self-control, they often have to stifle impatience because of lack of progress or mistakes made by others. They are action-oriented, organized, and analytical. Therefore, they have difficulty tolerating people or situations that are slow moving, disorganized, or shortsighted. But they view their battle for emotional control as a test of strength. They play to win and do.

When questioned about major mistakes made during their tenure as presidents, these CEO's were silent while groping for answers. After reflecting, half of the interviewees could not recall a single incident, and those who responded provided scenarios related to minor problems. Apparently, real crises rarely occur because the most effective academic leaders do not operate with a mistake mind-set when dealing with obstacles and unrealized opportunities. Rather than ignoring potentially damaging situations, they analyze the variables and take action. Unquestionably, obstacles are not the focal point for these leaders. Instead, it is their up-front, decisive manner in dealing with challenges that makes the difference.

CREDENTIALS AND EXPERIENCE

During this phase of the interviews, we wanted to identify the credentials and experiences most useful to these highly successful presidents. So we asked the presidents which academic credential is the most important and what early experiences made them think they could be successful leaders.

Most, by far, mentioned the earned doctorate as their most important credential because it lends credibility to leaders in an academic setting. Also, some presidents feel that the PhD holds particular significance because it represents their first piece of professional scholarship.

Our next question regarding early leadership experiences yielded interesting comments. Although there were exceptions, most effective presidents began leading at an early age, emerging as adolescents who had confidence in their abilities, were comfortable in leadership positions, and accepted more responsibility than their peers. By assuming leadership positions early in life, the members of this elite group learned to take risks and motivate others to follow, whether as athletes, officers in clubs and organizations, or leaders of peer groups. During the maturation process, they were able to fine-tune their persuasive skills so that others enjoyed having them as leaders of the pack. From our discussions it appears that genuine leaders emerge and rise to the top by acquiring experiences and credentials necessary for effectiveness. As one university president says, "I think people who end up in leadership positions are people who wanted to get something done, started getting things done, and somebody noticed."

MOTIVES AND MOTIVATIONS

What would the interviewees be doing today if they had not become college presidents? Most say they would be teaching or educating people in a traditional academic setting or working in places not typically associated with higher education (churches, clinics, and so forth). However, the fact remains that they emerged as leaders and accepted responsibility associated with the abilities they possess.

Once these leaders entered the field of higher education administration, their ascension to the presidential suite progressed naturally. After holding other administrative posts earlier in their careers, they realized that they had ideas about how to operate a college or university. Because others also believed in their ideas, these presidents got the opportunity to test their ability.

What motivates these presidents to stay in a position that is often thankless and where one's best efforts cannot possibly make everyone happy? Without hesitation, the 18 most effective presidents say they accepted the position because it is a challenge and they believe they have something to contribute to the higher education community. The job sounded interesting, exciting, and somewhat mysterious. Interestingly, few members of this elite group sought to be a president. Initially they did not aspire to the presidency. It was something that just happened.

They continue to be motivated by their presidencies because they feel good about the things they are accomplishing. They are still fascinated with the job that exposes them to a wide range of people and activities. During talks with these presidents, there was excitement in the air. They are motivated to perform at peak levels, not only because there is pride associated with past accomplishments but also because there are many things left to do. The words of a 2-year college president echo the sentiment of the group: "What keeps me going now is what happens on the campus every day: the life on the campus, the spirit and enthusiasm of the students, and the things the faculty want to do."

ACADEMIC TRAINING FOR THE PRESIDENCY

If these 18 presidents were designing a training program for people who want to be a college president, what would they include in the program? Although their answers to this question are diverse, we find three categories of responses: general education courses, administrative courses, and practical experiences.

As a group, the most effective presidents are concerned about the content of traditional educational administration programs. They believe that such programs should include a general education curriculum and should focus less on the how-to's. Many of them favor an interdisciplinary approach that promotes breadth of learning.

They identify several common areas of study as being critical to presidential success, particularly disciplines that encourage an understanding of oneself in relation to other people and past events. So it is not surprising that these presidents most often mention the study of history and historical literature as being an integral part of leadership training. They feel that, by being aware of the past, we can better cope with the future. We can learn from the successes and failures of others who have shaped our world. Furthermore, most of the presidents believe that courses in political science, sociology, human relations, and anthropology are important because they lead to an appreciation of time and the development of human societies. They also strongly believe that aspiring presidents should focus on areas that promote analytical thinking and the ability to express oneself in a clear, concise manner. Several of those interviewed also noted that aspiring presidents should develop a respect for language.

Some presidents favor the case-study approach as a way of training a chief executive officer. By reading and discussing specific cases in an open forum, students can see the complexity of issues and are encouraged to weigh the pros and cons of possible problem-solving strategies. In so doing, they can explore management theories and practices, as well as values that affect decision-making processes.

Finally, interviewed presidents feel that there should be a strong component of learning-by-doing. They favor internships or master–apprentice relationships as a way of exposing aspiring presidents to budgetary procedures, policy development, information transmission and control, and personnel issues.

Actually, the most effective academic leaders believe that each of these components plays an important role in developing future administrators. But they think that training per se is a misnomer because it is simply a piece of the larger puzzle known as the learning experience. According to these presidents, a person who possesses the appropriate raw material, has a solid educational background, enjoys work, and continues to grow both personally and professionally can acquire appropriate experiences leading to the development of strong administrative skills and effective leadership abilities.

THE PROACTIVE LEADER

After talking with this group of college presidents, we have little doubt as to why their associates view them as being among the most effective academic leaders in the country. They are the torchbearers who determine the course of higher education through their commitment to learning and personal improvement.

The leadership style of the 18 interviewees reflects their overriding concern for improving the human condition and the worth of the individual. They value others so much that they seldom make decisions without first considering the impact that action will have on various players. As leaders, they exhibit a strong sense of self, a belief in their ability to accomplish established goals, and such a strong belief in others that they allow co-workers a high degree of freedom to act. These presidents surround themselves with talented, creative people and give them the latitude to perform assigned duties as they see fit.

The leadership style of the most effective presidents is proactive: They seize and capitalize on opportunities by being persistent in pursuing their goals. They establish institutional priorities with great care through intense planning and preparation, and they seek advice from people at many levels in the organization during the planning process. Yet these presidents realize that they must make the hard decisions. And they act accordingly. They reward those who are creative and engage in calculated risk taking. Hence, the most effective presidents create an environment that is fertile for creative minds. Coupled with their uncompromised intensity for work and an appreciation for the efforts of others is a sense of humor, especially at times when others find little reason to laugh.

We find that these 18 presidents possess exceptional human relations skills. They are warm and caring individuals who treat others respectfully, regardless of their position in the organization. They are charismatic, but they use power to influence, persuade, and garner support rather than as a tool to manipulate subordinates against their will. In fact, they rarely pursue personal gain, as shown by their willingness to share the limelight with others responsible for successes.

The most effective presidents are leaders who have dreams and visions for their institutions. Obstacles do not cause them to abandon their dreams but are hurdles to be jumped before they can achieve goals. These effective presidents continue to meet challenges because there is so much more to accomplish. There are always more dreams to be realized, and there is always one more hill to climb.

·6·

Profiling the Effective College President: A Summary

There is an acknowledged leadership crisis in America that pervades all types of institutions, from government and education in general to higher education in particular. As Burns (1978) forthrightly asserts, "The call for leadership is one of the keynotes of our time" (p. 45). Yet, thus far, the only response has been an echo.

Society has lost faith in many of its institutions and their leaders. Thus, there are funding dilemmas, image problems, accountability issues, and a general lack of confidence in the ability of organized groups to work effectively and efficiently. With this diminution of faith and support, higher education, an instrument of society, has suffered seemingly irreparable setbacks.

We are now at a critical juncture in the history of higher edu-

99

cation. Unless effective leaders are found in abundance to lead America's institutions, higher education as we know it today might not survive. We might have been lulled into complacency by those who believe that committees can run institutions or that presidents are merely ceremonial figures who preside over graduation and retirement ceremonies. Indeed, we must erase these notions from our minds if we expect to educate future generations of students or if we intend to improve the quality of life through research and service. Unless we allow leaders to take charge of the enterprise and to chart a sound course for the future, higher education institutions might not remain viable places in which to think and grow.

At almost every higher education meeting held today, someone inevitably mentions the lack of strong presidential leadership as the root of higher education's problems. Numerous current and emeritus presidents have pointed to the need to strengthen the position of president. Researchers have repeatedly verified the fact that the president is the pivotal figure in institutional success. And hundreds of scholars of the presidency have suggested that the president cannot merely manage—he or she must lead. As Chaffee, Whetten, and Cameron (1983) point out, a college or university cannot "rise above the level of the president's leadership" (p. 219). However, although knowing that we need strong leaders in campus chief executive offices, we have been unable or unwilling to do anything about the problem. We have done little to improve the presidential appointment process. At many institutions, governance is an egalitarian shambles, and presidential evaluation techniques seem bound to reduce the president's leadership potential.

Why do we find ourselves in this quagmire? Perhaps the situation exists because we have allowed the governance of higher education to be democratized to the point that we really do not know who is in charge. And there are even those among us who do not want anyone to be in charge. Leadership in higher education now means involvement, and the decision-making process is constrained by the need to manage by consensus and yield to the will of the majority. Though everyone recognizes that an organization must have a leader, most people today, particularly in academia, want to have a hand in calling the shots. Consequently, we have come to expect leaders to bow to the wishes of constituents. Special-interest groups lobby for favors; trustees allow their political alliances to take priority over their responsibilities to the institution; and presidents must frequently jockey for power that is based on the strength of the group supporting a position rather than on what is best for higher education.

At times, it seems that trustees have lost sight of the fact that they must select the best president they can find for their institution, no matter what others might think. Unfortunately, in their efforts to respond to constituent demands, they have allowed a participatory governance mentality to influence the presidential selection process dramatically. They allow anyone who might possibly be affected by the president's actions, which includes the universe, to serve on the selection committee. Frequently, these constituent group representatives look for candidates who will advance their causes, which in the long run might not be in the institution's best interests. Thus, during the selection process, the goal of selecting the best president for the institution often gets lost in the ensuing personal power struggle among committee members. National organizations reinforce the condition through meetings and publications that instruct governing boards to include everyone in the presidential selection process, so that no one is really responsible. The process becomes more important than the result, and the faceless president emerges.

Another procedure that affects the trustees' ability to select the best presidential candidate is the lack of confidentiality during the screening process. The openness of the search often causes sitting presidents to remove their names from applicant pools because they fear erosion of existing, and often delicately balanced, power bases. In such a morass, the strong, decisive leader has little chance of being selected.

If, by chance, the selection process produces a strong president, an array of seemingly uncontrollable factors affects his or her survival rate. For instance, if faculty and students have been allowed to assume they should have primacy in decision making, the forward-thinking, decisive leader is immobilized. Compounding the condition and further complicating the leadership environment is the increased regulation exercised by external agencies and the trend toward reliance on external funding for a substantial portion of an institution's operating expenses.

Thus, we see that, for the past 20 years, higher education has existed in an environment that values collegiality and extensive participant involvement more than strong leadership. As Bass (1985) notes, "Modern universities, particularly American public universities, as state agencies represent organizations in which transformational leadership is less likely to be seen" (pp. 159–160). A retired president of a state college supplies further evidence of this problem:

> Today the president is pretty much a "clerk of the works." He keeps track of government regulations, union negotiations, computer printouts, and whose ox is about to be gored. He doesn't need to have an idea in his head or the gumption to make a decision because that is all taken care of by one of a host of committees. If nothing ever gets done, there is no one to blame because the president is far out of sight behind all those committees. (Carbone, 1981, p. 78)

Such lethargic conditions might be acceptable during periods of prosperity and tranquility and at established institutions that are not significantly affected by the tides of the times, but during periods of change and stress the poorly led institution soon falters and fails.

If it is the president who ultimately determines the success or failure of an institution, we definitely need to know more about what it is that makes him or her effective. Are there certain leadership behaviors that separate successful from unsuccessful presidents? Are there any personal and professional traits that enhance a person's ability to be effective in a presidential position? The answer to these questions could have a profound impact on selecting, preparing, and developing future leaders of America's higher education institutions.

REVIEW OF THE PRESIDENTIAL PROFILE

Our study reveals that there *are* distinctive personal and professional traits that separate effective presidents from their representative counterparts. In fact, there are statistically significant differences between effective and representative presidents in over a dozen different areas, and there are definite patterns in several others. Although there are some differences in personal background, fortunately most of the variances occur in areas that an individual can control, for instance, the type of degrees earned and the emphasis placed on scholarly activity. The findings are, from our perspective, not only intriguing but also useful to those who are interested in the making of an effective college president.

Educational Experiences

In terms of educational background, effective presidents are more likely to have attended a private than a public institution for their doctoral-level preparation. In addition, they are less likely to have received a master's degree from a public institution or to have majored in business at the baccalaureate level.

As we thought about these statistically significant findings, we decided that the content and process of graduate educational experiences at private institutions might enhance leadership effectiveness. This might be true because of such factors as the emphasis on research, the individual attention a student gets, or other, less obvious, factors such as the environment itself. In terms of the baccalaureate major, we believe effective presidents are initially attracted to disciplines other than business perhaps because of their desire to obtain a broad-based view rather than a technical perspective on the world in which we live. Suffice it to say that these findings need additional study to determine why the relationships exist. But, on the basis of our interpretations, there are some interesting connections to consider as we try to identify experiences that enhance leadership effectiveness.

Professional Experiences

We note several differences in the professional arena between effective and representative presidents.

1. *Representative presidents assumed their initial presidency at a later age and have spent fewer years in their current positions than the effec-*

tive group. These findings suggest that effective presidents do not let any grass grow under their feet in terms of their ascension to the office of president. Their talent is quickly identified, and they either choose or are persuaded to enter the administrative ranks, and the presidency, at a relatively young age. In addition, we find that effective presidents tend to make substantial commitments to their institutions in terms of the number of years they preside over them. Perhaps this is because they recognize that change and strength are not developed overnight. They not only use their visionary insight to chart a course for the institution, but they also stay around long enough to see the results of their labor. Their longevity in office also suggests to us that they tend to be successful.

2. *Effective presidents are more likely to head institutions with larger student enrollments.* Specifically, effective presidents lead institutions with an average head count of 11,200, compared with 5,200 for representative presidents. In most cases, this could be a corroboration of the fact that it is easier to lead a larger organization; the resources available for presidents to use in enhancing their institutions' academic programs and in attracting high quality students reflect the institution's enrollment size. Without resources, even the most effective president cannot develop a track record of success.

3. *Representative presidents have worked fewer years outside the higher education environment than have effective presidents.* Conceivably, this diversity in professional experiences gives effective presidents an added, and needed, edge. They understand the factors that affect leadership in agencies other than higher education. Moreover, they have professional contacts in organizations outside of higher education and, thus, can enhance their institutional budgets, improve academic programming, or expand student recruiting efforts. Through these varied experiences, effective presidents have perhaps been able to use an eclectic approach in developing their leadership style. In other words, they have been able to test leadership behaviors in a variety of settings and now consistently use only those that have proven successful across the board.

4. *Effective presidents make a significant contribution to their fields* *by publishing more articles and books and by being involved in more professional organizations than representative presidents.* Moreover, their leadership is not restricted to the institutional setting because they tend to rise to positions of authority within their professional organizations. Therefore, it appears that effective presidents understand the importance of maintaining a record of scholarship even though they are no longer faculty members. They probably are not writing or conducting research in their doctoral disciplines, unless they happened to major in administration, because it is difficult to keep up with continuously evolving, technical fields. However, they share their knowledge of leadership through such vehicles as case studies, position papers, reaction papers, presentations at national or regional meetings, or books. Colleagues recognize their contributions and elect them to serve as either members or chairs of national boards or major national committees. Interestingly, effective presidents tend to be associated with the American Council on Education or with other national organizations having a primary focus on higher education. The national visibility and impact these organizations have on educational policy probably contribute to their place at the head of the list.

5. *Effective presidents command higher salaries than their representative counterparts.* Happily, all of their hard works pays off. Although money definitely does not motivate effective presidents to perform, their higher salaries point to the fact that others recognize their prowess and reward them for the dedication they have to the tasks at hand.

6. *There is a connection between the institutions granting degrees to effective presidents and the existence of effective presidential leadership within those institutions.* For instance, the four institutions that surfaced at the baccalaureate, master's, and doctoral levels as having trained many effective presidents (The University of Michigan, Yale University, Harvard University, and Vanderbilt University) were also headed by some of the most widely acclaimed presidents in the country (those nominated three times or more). Perhaps this is another confirmation of a linkage between effective presidential leadership and the academic quality of the institution's programs.

Personal Traits

There are also personal differences that separate effective from representative presidents.

1. *Representative presidents are younger than effective presidents, leading us to conclude that members of the effective group are more experienced leaders.* Although they enter office earlier, they stay longer. Unquestionably, developing the appropriate set of credentials takes both time and systematic planning.

2. *When compared with representative presidents, effective presidents are more likely to be associated with the independent political philosophy.* This reinforces the notion that effective presidents are free, unencumbered thinkers who do not wish to be labeled or constrained unnecessarily when they have to make decisions.

3. *Effective presidents did not come from homes with college-educated parents.* In fact, their parents generally did not graduate from high school. Interestingly, when compared with the representative sample, the mothers of effective presidents are less likely to have even attended high school. Perhaps the value their parents placed on education motivated them to succeed. That success probably influences them to work as hard as necessary to see that such opportunities for learning and growth remain available for others.

Thus, we see that effective presidents have a background that is different from that of representative presidents. Perhaps these findings will allow us to advise those who wish to be higher education's leaders about a career path. Also, we should probably look at what private institutions do at the graduate level that has such an overwhelming impact on leadership effectiveness. Given research in this area, public institutions might be able to implement new or improved training programs. This might make it easier to train a larger number of people who have the skills and knowledge to be effective presidents.

LEADERSHIP BEHAVIORS

Our research findings support the conclusion that effective college presidents behave in certain ways as leaders of their institutions. Their representative counterparts do not exhibit these behaviors as overtly.

1. *Effective presidents are completely and unabashedly committed to what they do.* They believe in higher education, they believe in the mission of their institutions, and they love their jobs. They embrace the philosophy that people should be able to become all they are capable of becoming and that higher education is one of the best vehicles for translating this philosophy into reality. Thus, they have a distinct vision for all of higher education, as well as for the particular institutions they head. They see the job of leading an institution as a calling or a mission rather than as a job. Perhaps that's why they can work almost 24 hours a day pursuing their goals. (Even if they are not actually in the office, they probably are either thinking or dreaming about some aspect of their work.) They work hard to establish an environment where everyone benefits and where the institution contributes to a better life for everyone. In so doing, they are willing to make decisions that in the long run will benefit higher education, society, or both but that might adversely affect their institutions in the short run. Indeed, their actions speak louder than their words.

2. *Effective presidents focus on winning.* They are not content to just serve as chief executive officer. They are determined to make a difference in the life of the institution, and they will not be satisfied until they have achieved their goals. This mind-set pervades everything they do and is fed by their high self-confidence. They know they can accomplish whatever they set out to do, so they never think about losing. In order to win consistently, they work extremely hard and are always well prepared.

3. *Effective presidents recognize that the job of being president is a tough one and that they cannot please all of the people all of the time.* Therefore, it is their inner strength that keeps them going and not whether or not they are liked by those they lead. For them, it is more important to be respected than it is to be popular. Indeed, they understand that, without the respect of the people involved, a leader has nothing. These presidents engender respect by the way they conduct themselves publicly: They maintain a delicate balance between openness and privacy, between being a buddy and being a strong leader, and between being prepared and being spontaneous in actions and words.

4. *Effective presidents are thoughtful and deliberate in their decision making, but they are not satisfied with the status quo.* Needless to say, they are willing to take calculated risks to move the institution forward and will do so, if necessary, with or without consensus from the people involved. But they take these risks only after carefully considering the consequences of their actions. They want their constituencies to know that they have their best interests in mind, and they do not want to appear to make decisions too quickly or haphazardly. We are not suggesting that effective presidents avoid seeking opinions and ideas from constituents. On the contrary, they consistently seek information from those to be affected by a decision. However, if they intuitively do not believe the recommendation that emerges from the group will maximize the potential of the institution, they will move in another direction. The ability to assume a strong, decisive stance requires confidence, stamina, and courage, traits that are also essential for effective presidential leadership.

As we talk about decision making, issues related to the use of power arise. Interestingly, we find that the power of effective presidents consistently equates with persuasion and personal charisma rather than with attempts to manipulate. Effective presidents recognize that it is much more important to convince people that actions under consideration are in their best interest than it is to tell them what they must do and believe. If they ever have to rely on their power to get things done, effective presidents know they will not be successful. Thus, although they have legitimate power, they resist using (and losing) it.

5. *Effective presidents believe in merit pay more strongly than the representative group.* Thus, their decisiveness and penchant for risk taking affect every area of institutional operations including salary administration. Effective presidents are willing to step forward and reward those who perform meritoriously. They recognize that an institution cannot achieve its goals if faculty and staff are content with mediocrity. Effective presidents certainly are not mediocre, and they associate with or surround themselves with only the best people. Although they know that a person's salary is not a major motivating force, they overtly reward superior performance, perhaps as a way of saying thank you.

6. *Effective presidents recognize that it is quicker and wiser to go directly to the root of a problem or the source of information than it is to* *be encumbered by the bureaucracy.* Therefore, they frequently telephone faculty, talk with unit directors, and appear in people's offices unannounced to get information or ask questions. Once again, they are unafraid to take the bull by the horns. They recognize that campus organizational structure is necessary, but they do not allow the structure to smother them. They let their vice presidents and deans know that they, as CEOs, may talk with people anywhere in the organization. Therefore, the entire college or university is their stage.

7. *Effective presidents do not surround themselves with yes-people.* They encourage people to think creatively and to consider alternatives that appear on the surface to be impossible. Through listening to people who think differently, effective presidents stretch and grow. They do not want people to parrot back to them what they think the president wants to hear. In fact, they highly regard those willing to establish a different agenda.

8. *Effective presidents have a sense of humor.* The workaholic nature of effective presidents, coupled with their high expectations of themselves and others, could be devastating if not managed appropriately. Fortunately, we find that, even though effective presidents are serious about their jobs and concerned about success, they enjoy having fun and laughing. They are extremely witty (another sign of their innate intelligence) and use humor as a way to ease tension.

9. *Effective presidents are deeply concerned about the welfare of the individual.* They believe in and respect people, and they want only the best for them. However, because of their action orientation, they occasionally appear to be impatient or less than thoughtful. At intervals, they have to put their personal feelings on hold, to make decisions that are best for the institution and higher education in general. They can and do call a spade a spade, even if this adversely affects people.

10. *Effective presidents exercise a great deal of self-control in dealing with others.* They try to be consistent and keep their emotions under control. They know their personal weaknesses, such as impatience and a tendency to lose their tempers when people have not performed up to their expectations. Moreover, they know that uncontrolled outbursts can create communication barriers and affect their associates' willingness to share information in the future. They struggle with their personal frailties. But, as in all other instances, they usually win the battles.

11. *Effective presidents do not believe in close collegial relationships as strongly as do representative presidents.* Effective presidents must keep their relationships with people in general on a friendly yet reserved basis, in order to make the hard decisions. They let their hair down with only a few close associates, perhaps because they understand the importance of maintaining some measure (if only an ounce) of mystique.

12. *Effective presidents exude strength, confidence, intelligence, insightfulness, and decisiveness.* This aura is not accidental, and they develop and maintain it through personal and professional planning. They are confident enough of themselves to share the credit for successes and to be concerned about substance rather than fluff.

For example, visibility is not something that effective presidents think about a great deal. They know that just being the chief executive officer of an institution leads to high visibility. They are always on stage. They do not seek visibility for personal gain but always focus on the exposure they need to ensure institutional success. Incidentally, they typically share the credit for a successful project with those who helped design and implement it. They do not hesitate to share the limelight with others, once again underscoring their own internal sense of self-confidence and self-worth.

13. *Effective presidents are not overly concerned about appearance.* It might appear to some people that we uncovered a contradictory finding: that representative presidents are more concerned about dressing well than are effective presidents. But we don't think so. Apparently, effective presidents recognize that their ideas and actions are more important than how they look. Effective presidents might be well dressed, but they aren't concerned about making the best-dressed list. They are more interested in being identified with an effective plan of action or with sound ideas.

A PRESIDENTIAL SNAPSHOT

Based on this new information regarding the leadership behavior of effective presidents, what kind of profile can we develop? We know that they are different in a number of ways from representative presidents. In our minds, we believe that the most important findings from our research are related to the fact that effective presidents, among other things, are

- Less collegial and more distant
- Less likely to be spontaneous in speech and actions
- Less restricted by organizational structure or by the consensus of those to be led
- Less likely to appear to make decisions easily
- More confident
- More inclined to rely on gaining respect than on being liked
- More inclined to take calculated risks
- More committed to an ideal or a vision than to an institution
- More inclined to work long hours
- More supportive of the controversial concept of merit pay
- More interested in encouraging people to think differently and creatively
- More likely to be concerned about higher education in general than with one institution

IMPLICATIONS: THE SO-WHAT QUESTIONS

These research findings lead us to conclude that there are significant differences in the way effective presidents lead their institutions, and these differences contribute to institutional and individual success. The results defy traditional wisdom about the college presidency. In general, effective presidents are not the collegial prototype. They are strong, action-oriented visionaries who act out of educated intuition.

Without question, these results should have a significant impact on the presidential selection process. Members of boards of trustees now have documented evidence that certain baseline characteristics should be present if an individual is to be an effective chief executive officer in higher education. Up to now, perhaps college and university governing boards have been looking for the wrong types of people to lead our colleges and universities. Or maybe, when a good candidate slipped through the selection process, many institutions had become so bureaucratized that they squelched the dynamism of the energetic president. Probably both situations have existed, but regardless, the results have been unfortunate. We hope that these research findings will provide board members with the ammunition needed to hire stronger leaders for their institutions.

Moreover, potential candidates for presidencies will be able to assess their own leadership behaviors to decide whether they approximate the newly established profile of the effective college president. If they do not feel comfortable displaying the identified behaviors and wish to be effective, they then have two alternatives: They can abandon their idea of becoming a president, or they can change their behaviors. Indeed, many of the leadership behaviors identified as being distinctive in effective college presidents are learned behaviors. Therefore, appropriate training and professional-development activities can enhance a person's leadership prowess.

We believe it is important for people associated with training programs in higher education administration to review our research results. They should consider the results when screening potential students and when helping determine academic experiences in which selected students should be involved. Obviously, academically oriented training programs should be individually tailored and should include internship or apprenticeship experiences and a heavy dose of the case-study approach to learning. In addition, the best training programs either build on a liberal arts education or include experiences designed to expose presidential candidates trained in professional fields to the various facets of the world in which we live: culture, history, sociology, art, music, and so on.

The position of campus president is arguably the toughest job in America, as well as one of the most important. We can have persons at the helm who are strong, decisive decision makers and who have a dream for a better tomorrow. We must encourage boards and others involved in the selection process to select people who exemplify characteristics that best serve this end. This calls for a thoughtful review of the role of the various players in institutional governance, to make effective leadership more, rather than less, possible. Undoubtedly college presidents will lead if we will let them.

References

American Council on Education, Association of Governing Boards of Universities and Colleges. (1986). *Deciding who shall lead: Recommendations for improving presidential searches.* Washington, DC: Author.

Argyris, C., & Cyert, R. M. (1980). *Leadership in the '80s: Essays on higher education.* Cambridge, MA: Institute for Educational Management.

Astin, A. W., & Scherrei, R. A. (1980). *Maximizing leadership effectiveness.* San Francisco: Jossey-Bass.

Bass, B. M. (1985). *Leadership and performance beyond expectations.* New York: Macmillan, Free Press.

Barr, C. V. (1981). *Profiles of American college presidents—1968 and 1980: A comparison.* Unpublished doctoral dissertation, Bowling Green State University, Bowling Green, OH.

Benezet, L. T., Katz, J., & Magnusson, F. W. (1981). *Style and substance leadership and the college presidency.* Washington, DC: American Council on Education.

Bennis, W. G., & Nanus, B. (1985). *Leaders: The strategies for taking charge.* New York: Harper & Row.

Bittel, L. R. (1984). *Leadership: The key to management success.* New York: Franklin Watts.

Blau, P. M., & Scott, W. R. (1962). *Formal organizations: A comparative approach.* San Francisco: Chandler Publishing.

Bolman, F. (1965). *How college presidents are chosen.* Washington, DC: American Council on Education.

Brooks, G. D., & Avila, J. F. (1974). A descriptive profile of junior college presidents. *Research in Higher Education, 2,* 145–150.

Burns, J. M. (1978). *Leadership.* New York: Harper & Row.

Cameron, K. S., & Whetten, D. A. (1983). *Organizational effectiveness: A comparison of multiple models.* New York: Academic Press.

Carbone, R. F. (1981). *Presidential passages: Former college presidents reflect on the splendor and agony of their careers.* Washington, DC: American Council on Education.

Carmichael, J. H. (1969). Origin and mobility of presidents. *Junior College Journal, 39*(8), 30–32.

Carp, F. M., Vitola, B. M., & McLanathan, F. L. (1963). Human relations knowledge and social set in supervisors. *Journal of Applied Psychology, 47,* 78–80.

Chaffee, E. E., Whetten, D. A., & Cameron, K. S. (1983). *Case studies in college strategy.* Boulder, CO: National Center for Higher Education Management Systems.

Cleven, W. A., & Fiedler, F. E. (1956). Interpersonal perceptions of open-hearth foremen and steel production. *Journal of Applied Psychology, 41,* 312–314.

Cohen, M. D., & March, J. G. (1986). *Leadership and ambiguity: The American college president.* Boston: Harvard Business School Press.

Corson, J. J. (1975). *The governance of colleges and universities: Modernizing structure and processes.* New York: McGraw-Hill.

Cowley, W. H. (1980). *Presidents, professors, and trustees: The evolution of American academic government.* San Francisco: Jossey-Bass.

Cox, A. J. (1985). *The making of the achiever: How to win distinction in your company.* New York: Dodd, Mead.

Dressel, P. L. (1981). *Administrative leadership.* San Francisco: Jossey-Bass.

Drucker, P. F. (1967). *The effective executive.* New York: Harper & Row.

Duea, J. (1981). The making of a president, higher education style. *Phi Delta Kappan, 62,* 501–503.

Epstein, L. D. (1974). *Governing the university: The campus and the public interest.* San Francisco: Jossey-Bass.

Enarson, H. L. (1984). The ethical imperative of the college presidency. *Educational Record, 65*(2), 24–26.

Ferrari, M. R. (1970). *Profiles of American college presidents.* Unpublished doctoral dissertation, Division of Research, Graduate School of Business Administration, Michigan State University, East Lansing, MI.

Fiedler, R. E. (1955). The influence of leader-keyman relations on combat crew effectiveness. *Journal of Abnormal Psychology, 51,* 227–235.

Fiedler, F. E. (1967). *A theory of leadership effectiveness.* New York: McGraw-Hill.

Fisher, J. L. (1984a). *The power of the presidency.* New York: ACE/Macmillan.

Fisher, J. L. (1984b). Presidents will lead—if we let them. *Journal of the Association of Governing Boards of Universities and Colleges Reports, 26*(4), 11–14.

Fisher, J. L. (1986). Presidential assessment: A better way. *Journal of the Association of Governing Boards of Universities and Colleges Reports, 28*(5), 16–21.

Fisher, J. L., & Quehl, G. H. (1984). Presidential assessment: Obstacle to leadership. *Change, 16*(4), 5–7.

Fleishman, E. A., & Peters, D. R. (1962). Interpersonal values, leadership attitudes and managerial success. *Personnel Psychology, 15*(2), 127–143.

Follett, M. P. (1940). *Dynamic administration.* New York: Harper & Row.

French, J. R. P., & Raven, B. (1959). The bases of social power. In D. Cartwright (Ed.), *Studies in social power* (pp. 150–167). Ann Arbor: University of Michigan, Institute for Social Research, Research Center for Group Dynamics.

Gardner, J. W. (1986a). *The heart of the matter: Leader-constituent interaction.* Leadership Papers/3. Washington, DC: Independent Sector.

Gardner, J. W. (1986b). *Leadership and power.* Leadership Papers/4. Washington, DC: Independent Sector.

Gardner, R. G., & Brown, M. D. (1973). *Personal characteristics of community college presidents.* (ERIC Document Reproduction Service No. ED 104 456)

Gerth, H. H., & Mills, C. W. (Eds.). (1946). *From Max Weber: Essays in sociology.* New York: Oxford University Press.

Gilley, J. W., Fulmer, K. A., & Reithlingshoefer, S. J. (1986). *Searching for academic excellence: Twenty colleges and universities on the move and their leaders.* New York: ACE/Macmillan.

Gilli, A. C., Sr. (1976). *The community junior college presidency: An inquiry.* University Park, PA: Department of Vocational Education, Pennsylvania State University. (ERIC Document Reproduction Service No. ED 123 469)

Greenleaf, R. K. (1977). *Servant leadership.* New York: Paulist Press.

Hesburgh, T. (1979). The college presidency: Life between a rock and a hard place. *Change, 11*(4), 43–47.

Higher education directory (1984). Washington, DC: Higher Education Publications, Inc.

Hill, R. (1984). From war room to boardroom: Professional soldiers excelling as managers. *International Management, 39*(4), 23–28.

Hise, R. T., & McDaniel, S. W. (1985). Using CEO profiles in executive career planning. *Managerial Planning, 33*(5), 48–51.

Ingraham, M. H. (1968). *The mirror of brass: The compensation and working conditions of college and university administrators.* Madison, WI: University of Wisconsin Press.

Jenkins, W. O. (1947). A review of leadership studies with particular reference to military problems. *Psychological Bulletin, 44,* 54–79.

Johnson, J. A., & Drewry, G. N. (1982). *A profile of faculty of doctoral programs in the study of higher education in the United States.* University, AL: Institute of Higher Education Research and Services.

Kamm, R. B. (1982). *Leadership for leadership: Number one priority for presidents and other university administrators.* Washington, DC: University Press of America.

Katz, D. (1973). Patterns of leadership. In J. N. Knutson (Ed.), *Handbook of Political Psychology.* San Francisco: Jossey-Bass.

Katz, R. L. (1974). Skills of an effective administrator. *Harvard Business Review, 52*(5), 90–102.

Kauffman, J. F. (1984). Profile of the presidency in the next decade. *Educational Record, 65,* 6–10.

Keim, M. C. (1983). Exemplary graduate programs in higher education. *Educational Research Quarterly, 8*(3), 4–11.

Kerr, C. (1984). *Presidents make a difference: Strengthening leadership in colleges and universities: A report of the commission on strengthening presidential leadership.* Washington, DC: Association of Governing Boards of Universities and Colleges.

Kotter, J. P. (1977). Power, dependence, and effective management. *Harvard Business Review, 55*(4), 125–136.

Kotter, J. P. (1982). *The general managers.* New York: Macmillan, Free Press.

Laney, J. T. (1984). The moral authority of the college or university president. *Educational Record, 65*(2), 17–19.

Levinson, H. (1980). Criteria for choosing chief executives. *Harvard Business Review, 58*(4), 113–120.

Lowell, A. L. (1938). *What a university president has learned.* New York: Macmillan.

Maslow, A. H. (1970). *Motivation and personality.* New York: Harper & Row.

McClelland, D. C., & Burnham, D. H. (1976). Power is the great motivator. *Harvard Business Review, 54*(2), 100–110.

McDonagh, E. C., Schuerman, M. C., & Schuerman, L. A. (1970). Academic characteristics of presidents of major American universities. *Sociology and Social Research, 54,* 356–370.

Miller, E. L. (1983). University leaders: Having style rather than simply a style. *Change, 15*(1), 10–11.

Millett, J. D. (1962). *The academic community: An essay on organization.* New York: McGraw-Hill.

Millett, J. D. (1978). *New structures of campus power.* San Francisco: Jossey-Bass.

Moore, K. M., Salimbene, A. M., Marlier, J. D., & Bragg, S. M. (1983). The structure of presidents' and deans' careers. *Journal of Higher Education, 54,* 500–515.

Mortimer, K. P., & McConnell, T. R. (1978). *Sharing authority effectively.* San Francisco: Jossey-Bass.

Nason, J. W. (1980). *Presidential assessment: A challenge to college and university leadership.* Washington, DC: Association of Governing Boards of Universities and Colleges.

Nason, J. W. (1984). *Presidential search: A guide to the process of selecting and appointing college and university presidents.* Washington, DC: Association of Governing Boards of Universities and Colleges.

Ostar, R. H. (1983). *Myths and realities. 1983 report on the AASCU presidential spouses.* Washington, DC: American Association of State Colleges and Universities.

Peck, R. D. (1983). The entrepreneurial college presidency. *Educational Record, 64*(1), 18–25.

Peters, T., & Austin, N. (1985). *A passion for excellence: The leadership difference.* New York: Random House.

Peters, T. J., & Waterman, R. H., Jr. (1982). *In search of excellence: Lessons from America's best-run companies.* New York: Harper & Row.

Prator, R. (1963). *The college president.* Washington, DC: Center for Applied Research in Education.

Pray, F. C. (1979, May/June). The president as a "reasonable adventurer". Washington, DC: *Association of Governing Boards of Universities and Colleges,* pp. 45–48.

Pruitt, G. (1974). *Blueprint for leadership: The American college presidency.* Unpublished doctoral dissertation, Union for Experimenting Colleges and Universities, Cincinnati.

Richman, B. M., & Farmer, R. N. (1974). *Leadership, goals, and power in higher education: A contingency and open-system approach to effective management.* San Francisco: Jossey-Bass.

Robinson, J. A. (1986). Lieutenants to learning: A bibliography of participant-observation by university presidents. *Mershon Center Quarterly Report, 10*(4), 1–13.

Rubin, I. M., & Goldman, M. (1968). An open system model of leadership performance. *Organizational Behavior and Human Performance, 3,* 143–156.

Ryan, J. W. (1984). The mosaic of the college and university presidency. *Educational Record, 65*(2), 20–22.

Sammartino, P. (1982). *The president of a small college.* East Brunswick, NJ: Corwall Books.

SAS Institute Inc. (1985). *SAS user's guide: Statistics, version 5 edition.* Cary, NC: Author.

Selznick, P. (1957). *Leadership in administration: A sociological interpretation.* Evanston, IL: Row, Peterson.

Shaw, E. P. (1965). The social distance factor and management. *Personnel Administration, 28*(1), 29–31.

Shepherd, C., & Weschler, I. R. (1955). The relationship between three interpersonal variables, and communication effectiveness: A pilot study. *Sociometry, 18*(2), 103–110.

Stadtman, V. A. (1980). *Academic adaptations: Higher education prepares for the 1980s and 1990s.* San Francisco: Jossey-Bass.

Stogdill, R. M. (1948). Personal factors associated with leadership: A survey of the literature. *Journal of Psychology, 25,* 35–71.

Stogdill, R. M. (1974). *Handbook of leadership: A survey of theory and research.* New York: Macmillan, Free Press.

Stoke, H. W. (1959). *The American college president.* New York: Harper.

Szilagy, A. D., Jr., & Wallace, M. J., Jr. (1980). *Organizational behavior and performance.* Santa Monica: Goodyear.

Tead, O. (1951). *The art of administration.* New York: McGraw-Hill.

Thwing, C. F. (1926). *The college president.* New York: Macmillan.

Townsend, R. (1985). Townsend's third degree in leadership. *Across the Board, 22*(6), 48–52.

Vaughan, G. B. (1986). *The community college presidency.* New York: ACE/Macmillan.

Wakin, E. (1985). The CEO as consumate communicator. *Today's Office, 19*(12), 51–54.

Walker, D. E. (1981). *The effective administrator.* San Francisco: Jossey-Bass.

Weathersby, G. (1973). Purpose, persuasion, backbone, and spunk. In W. W. Jellema (Ed.), *Efficient college management* (pp. 3–10). San Francisco: Jossey-Bass.

Weiss, A. (1984). Simple truths of Japanese manufacturing. *Harvard Business Review, 62*(4), 119–125.

Wells, H. B. (1980). *Being lucky: Reminiscences and reflections.* Bloomington, IN: Indiana University Press.

Wenrich, J. W. (1980). Can the president be all things to all people? *Community and Junior College Journal, 51*(2), 36–40.

What makes top executives tick? (1983, December). *Association Management,* pp. 123–125.

Whetten, D. A. (1984). Effective administrators: Good management on the college campus. *Change, 16*(8), 38–43.

Whetten, D. A., & Cameron, K. S. (1985). Administrative effectiveness in higher education. *Review of Higher Education, 9,* 35–49.

APPENDIX
·A·

Fisher/Tack Effective Leadership Inventory (Pilot)

Please react to the following statements about your own characteristics as a leader by circling the appropriate responses. Your responses should represent your perceptions of yourself as a leader.

SA = Strongly Agree   A = Agree   NO = No Opinion
D = Disagree   SD = Strongly Disagree

The effective president:

1. Is sometimes viewed as hard-nosed.   SA   A   NO   D   SD

2. Believes that what the leader stands for is more important than what he/she does.   SA   A   NO   D   SD

3. Maintains that effective leadership is significantly based on authority.   SA   A   NO   D   SD

4. Never uses coercion as a method of influence.   SA   A   NO   D   SD

The effective president:

5. Believes that a leader should be perceived as somewhat distant from followers.   SA   A   NO   D   SD

6. Believes that the respect of those to be led is essential.   SA   A   NO   D   SD

7. Is more concerned about impact than personal achievement or affiliation.   SA   A   NO   D   SD

8. Believes that effective leaders take risks.   SA   A   NO   D   SD

9. Believes that good management is the main characteristic of effective leadership.   SA   A   NO   D   SD

10. Is primarily concerned about being liked.   SA   A   NO   D   SD

11. Believes that voluntary compliance is the only form of effective leadership.   SA   A   NO   D   SD

12. Would rather be right than loved.   SA   A   NO   D   SD

13. Believes in deep participation in corporate meetings.   SA   A   NO   D   SD

14. Spends a lot of time out of the office.   SA   A   NO   D   SD

15. Believes in high personal visibility.   SA   A   NO   D   SD

16. Bases final decisions on consensus.   SA   A   NO   D   SD

17. Is more committed to service than profit.   SA   A   NO   D   SD

18. Believes in corporate ceremonial activity.   SA   A   NO   D   SD

19. Retains final authority over all decision making.   SA   A   NO   D   SD

20. Eschews the limelight.   SA   A   NO   D   SD

21. Tries to achieve consensus.   SA   A   NO   D   SD

22. Believes in traditional perquisites in office.   SA   A   NO   D   SD

The effective president:

23. Shares the credit for successes.	SA	A	NO	D	SD
24. Grants associates leadership opportunities.	SA	A	NO	D	SD
25. Accepts responsibility for corporate failures.	SA	A	NO	D	SD
26. Views leadership as a personal quality.	SA	A	NO	D	SD
27. Believes in organizational structure.	SA	A	NO	D	SD
28. Believes that leadership roles are often lonely.	SA	A	NO	D	SD
29. Likes to be called by first name.	SA	A	NO	D	SD
30. Would rather not have a personal driver.	SA	A	NO	D	SD
31. Encourages others in the corporation to serve as group leaders during his/her presence.	SA	A	NO	D	SD
32. Uses retreats as a means of corporate development.	SA	A	NO	D	SD
33. Believes that the leader should be perceived as self-confident.	SA	A	NO	D	SD
34. Is a visionary.	SA	A	NO	D	SD
35. Loves debate.	SA	A	NO	D	SD
36. At times enjoys controversy.	SA	A	NO	D	SD
37. Believes the leader is most effective who is best liked.	SA	A	NO	D	SD
38. Believes in close collegial relationships.	SA	A	NO	D	SD
39. Believes that knowledge is the primary key to power.	SA	A	NO	D	SD
40. Believes that high ideals and a sense of reverence are prerequisites for effective leadership.	SA	A	NO	D	SD
41. Believes that leaders serve the people.	SA	A	NO	D	SD

The effective president:

42. Believes that one's spiritual nature significantly contributes to the meaning of life.   SA A NO D SD

43. Believes in merit pay.   SA A NO D SD

44. Is sometimes viewed as assertive.   SA A NO D SD

45. Is rarely in keeping with the status quo.   SA A NO D SD

46. Believes that speaking from an elevated platform lends impact to a presentation.   SA A NO D SD

47. Establishes organizational goals with the primary aim of stretching and challenging all staff.   SA A NO D SD

48. Believes that corporate goals will be achieved when individual and organizational goals are both served.   SA A NO D SD

49. Values loyalty as much as competence.   SA A NO D SD

50. Carries out disciplinary action in such a way that employees do not feel anxious.   SA A NO D SD

51. Believes that the ability to inspire trust and confidence is the most important skill of the effective leader.   SA A NO D SD

52. Believes that colleagueship is an essential ingredient in effective leadership.   SA A NO D SD

53. Delegates responsibility and authority to subordinates.   SA A NO D SD

54. Believes that after being appointed to a leadership position one should behave the same as before.   SA A NO D SD

55. Believes that too much informal behavior on the part of the leader reduces effectiveness.   SA A NO D SD

The effective president:

56. Believes in the value of one-on-one meetings. SA A NO D SD

57. Finds his or her spouse helpful in corporate decision making. SA A NO D SD

58. Views social occasions as opportunities for business discussions. SA A NO D SD

59. Maintains a measure of mystique. SA A NO D SD

60. Uses large social functions to advance the corporation. SA A NO D SD

61. Chooses another CEO as a confidant. SA A NO D SD

62. Has frequently risked the displeasure of those in power. SA A NO D SD

63. Believes in community involvement. SA A NO D SD

64. Is driven by the opinions of others in important positions. SA A NO D SD

65. Believes that merit will out. SA A NO D SD

66. Enjoys being with the "little" people. SA A NO D SD

67. Appreciates the importance of details. SA A NO D SD

68. Always appears energetic. SA A NO D SD

69. Is a nitpicker. SA A NO D SD

70. Is often viewed as a loner. SA A NO D SD

71. Believes in social and professional "distance." SA A NO D SD

72. Likes to be perceived as a colleague. SA A NO D SD

73. Counts committee meetings as mistakes. SA A NO D SD

74. Tends to act out of educated intuition. SA A NO D SD

75. Often has a troubled personal life. SA A NO D SD

76. Includes executives from all corporate levels in "cabinet" meetings. SA A NO D SD

The effective president:

77. Would rather be viewed as a strong leader than a good colleague.	SA	A	NO	D	SD
78. Accepts losses gracefully.	SA	A	NO	D	SD
79. Tends to work long hours.	SA	A	NO	D	SD
80. Is rarely at peace.	SA	A	NO	D	SD
81. Is consumed by the cause.	SA	A	NO	D	SD
82. Often likes people who are different.	SA	A	NO	D	SD
83. Is an effective speaker.	SA	A	NO	D	SD
84. Only occasionally speaks spontaneously.	SA	A	NO	D	SD
85. Joins lots of clubs.	SA	A	NO	D	SD
86. Is warm and affable.	SA	A	NO	D	SD
87. Has a large number of close friends.	SA	A	NO	D	SD
88. Is often seen as somewhat aloof.	SA	A	NO	D	SD
89. Dresses well.	SA	A	NO	D	SD
90. Is usually caught up in global issues.	SA	A	NO	D	SD
91. Deeply cares about the welfare of the individual.	SA	A	NO	D	SD
92. Believes in the corporation at all costs.	SA	A	NO	D	SD
93. Is more inclined toward action than planning.	SA	A	NO	D	SD
94. Encourages creative types even though often in disagreement.	SA	A	NO	D	SD
95. Appears to make decisions easily.	SA	A	NO	D	SD
96. Appears confident even when in doubt.	SA	A	NO	D	SD
97. Feels the need to know virtually everything about the activities of the corporation.	SA	A	NO	D	SD
98. Is quick to give praise and credit.	SA	A	NO	D	SD
99. Views him/herself and the corporation as one.	SA	A	NO	D	SD
100. Believes in presidential power.	SA	A	NO	D	SD

The effective president:

101.	Would rather be respected than liked.	SA	A	NO	D	SD
102.	Would rather be influential than professionally admired.	SA	A	NO	D	SD
103.	Enjoys stirring things up.	SA	A	NO	D	SD
104.	Tends to operate at the precipice.	SA	A	NO	D	SD
105.	Is poetic by nature.	SA	A	NO	D	SD
106.	Is rarely viewed as flamboyant.	SA	A	NO	D	SD
107.	Is very careful.	SA	A	NO	D	SD
108.	Appears to enjoy the perquisites of office.	SA	A	NO	D	SD
109.	Smiles a lot.	SA	A	NO	D	SD

In the space provided please record any comments you have about the questionnaire in general or any specific statements. Your comments will be used to strengthen the instrument prior to its administration to a broader audience of college presidents.

Please return this instrument to:
Bowling Green State University
ATTN: Dr. Martha W. Tack, EDAS
Bowling Green, OH 43403

APPENDIX
·*B*·

Instrument Development

The Fisher/Tack Effective Leadership Inventory consists of three sections: Part I: Personal Attitudes and Leadership Style; Part II: Professional Data; and Part III: Personal Information. We included questions in Parts II and III after having reviewed other questionnaires and U.S. Census Bureau instrumentation. But we had no models to use in developing the statements for Part I dealing with leadership behaviors. Therefore, we developed a set of 109 statements about leadership behaviors based on our own knowledge and available literature. We then pilot tested these items, using a stratified random sample of 400 current 2-year, 4-year, public, and private college presidents from throughout the country. After one follow-up, 256 responded (64% of the population surveyed).

Items were selected for Part I of the Fisher/Tack Effective Leadership Inventory, using both subjective and objective methods. By analyzing the nature and frequency of respondents' comments ($N = 256$), we reduced the number of items contained on the pilot questionnaire from 109 to 64 items. Data were then processed using the SAS software system (SAS Institute, Inc., 1985).

To gain insight into the relationships between the independent and dependent variables and to reduce further the number of items contained on the questionnaire, a stepwise regression procedure was used. All items with an R^2 value greater than .40 ($n = 10$) were deleted during this phase of the instrument development.

A principal-components factor analysis procedure was performed on the remaining 54 items. This analysis identified 20 factors; however, only 6 of the 20 factors (1, 2, 3, 4, 7, and 11) had significant loadings ($r > .29$) of 3 or more items, for a total of 42 items.

To adhere to the predetermined ceiling of 40 items on the final questionnaire, 2 of the 42 items were deleted because of comments from pilot-test respondents (item 107 from factor 3 and item 32 from factor 11). Because factor 11 met the criteria of having three or more items with significant loadings before the deletion of item 32, the remaining two items that loaded in the factor (78 and 84) were retained. In our opinion, these items were most closely related to items contained in factor 1; therefore, they were included in the factor 1 grouping.

For scoring purposes, the signs for factor loadings were followed, except for items contained in factor 4. In this case, the signs for items 10, 38, 61, 82, 89, 102, and 106 were reversed, that is, positive to negative and negative to positive. These reversals were made on the basis of the review of current literature pertaining to behaviors of effective leaders. Because the factors are independent, the reversals did not have an impact on the other four factors nor any overall effect on the pattern of responses in factor 4.

Because items were not scored dichotomously, we used Cronbach's Coefficient Alpha to determine internal consistency for each of the five factors. Reliability coefficients are as follows: Factor 1, $\alpha = .63$; factor 2, $\alpha = .51$; factor 3, $\alpha = .52$; and factor 4, $\alpha = .10$. Calculations for factor 7 resulted in a negative number, which indicates zero internal consistency reliability.

After completing the statistical procedures, we labeled factors in the following manner:

Factor 1: Management Style Index

Item 6. Believes that the respect of those to be led is essential.

Item 8. Believes that effective leaders take risks.

Item 21. Tries to achieve consensus.

Item 27. Believes in organizational structure.

Item 33. Believes that the leader should be perceived as self-confident.

Item 43. Believes in merit pay.

Item 44. Is sometimes viewed as assertive.

Item 53. Delegates responsibility and authority to subordinates.

Item 56. Believes in the value of one-on-one meetings.

Item 63. Believes in community involvement.

Item 68. Always appears energetic.

†Item 73. Counts committee meetings as mistakes.

Item 78. Accepts losses gracefully.

Item 79. Tends to work long hours.

Item 84. Only occasionally speaks spontaneously.

Item 86. Is warm and affable.

Item 91. Deeply cares about the welfare of the individual.

Item 94. Encourages creative types even though often in disagreement.

Factor 2: Human Relations Index

Item 1. Is sometimes viewed as hard-nosed.

†Item 41. Believes that leaders serve the people.

Item 59. Maintains a measure of mystique.

Item 60. Uses large social functions to advance the corporation.

Item 70. Is often viewed as a loner.

Item 77. Would rather be viewed as a strong leader than a good colleague.

Item 88. If often seen as somewhat aloof.

Item 103. Enjoys stirring things up.

Factor 3: Image Index

Item 96. Appears confident even when in doubt.

Item 99. Views him/herself and the corporation as one.

---

†Reversed items

Item 108. Appears to enjoy the perquisites of office.

Item 109. Smiles a lot.

Factor 4: Social Reference Index

†*Item 10.*   Is primarily concerned about being liked.

†*Item 38.*   Believes in close collegial relationships.

†*Item 61.*   Chooses another CEO as a confidant.

†*Item 82.*   Often likes people who are different.

Item 89.   Dresses well.

†*Item 102.* Would rather be influential than professionally admired.

Item 106. Is rarely viewed as flamboyant.

Factor 7: Confidence Index

†*Item 45.*   Is rarely in keeping with the status quo.

Item 92.   Believes in the corporation at all costs.

†*Item 95.*   Appears to make decisions easily.

APPENDIX

·*C*·

Factor Analysis: Fisher/Tack Effective Leadership Inventory

ITEM	1	2	3	4	5	6	7	8	9	10
1.	.15	.43	−.19	−.09	.23	−.18	−.11	.13	−.10	.11
6.	.47	−.14	.01	.13	−.01	.07	.16	.11	.10	−.01
8.	.59	.05	−.29	−.09	−.03	−.24	−.14	.11	.07	.09
† 10.	.18	−.14	.22	.42	.01	.04	.17	.23	.28	−.22
21.	.37	−.19	−.13	.28	.09	.18	−.02	.25	.10	.12
26.	.19	.08	.33	−.09	.08	−.05	−.00	.23	−.25	.03
27.	.38	.06	−.08	−.14	.17	−.33	.28	.03	.08	.06
28.	.41	.13	.07	−.20	.47	.14	.11	.19	.22	−.07
32.	.32	−.19	−.21	.25	−.13	.08	.16	−.08	.05	−.15
33.	.50	.15	−.10	−.08	−.18	−.02	−.11	.10	.02	−.09
† 38.	.15	−.34	.02	.45	.27	−.06	.26	.09	.00	.09
† 41.	.31	−.39	−.01	−.12	.28	.31	−.07	−.00	−.21	.17
43.	.44	.04	−.05	−.02	.36	−.01	−.20	−.33	−.01	−.27
44.	.41	.26	−.22	−.06	.16	.02	−.30	−.19	.01	.05
† 45.	.11	.18	−.00	−.02	−.20	−.11	−.42	.21	.29	.27
48.	.19	−.14	−.06	−.18	.25	.08	−.01	.27	−.10	−.01
53.	.45	−.30	−.30	−.01	−.15	−.30	.09	.07	.10	−.03
56.	.47	−.07	.01	−.13	−.29	−.17	.14	.25	−.00	.17
59.	.20	.38	.09	.04	.02	.25	.04	−.17	−.00	−.18
60.	.28	.34	−.23	.23	.01	−.17	.01	−.25	−.07	−.32
† 61.	.22	−.01	−.01	.29	−.15	−.03	.07	.08	.16	−.24
63.	.55	−.29	−.04	−.06	−.20	.01	−.07	.07	.11	.02
67.	.21	.02	−.06	−.28	−.01	−.04	.10	−.47	.10	.27
68.	.31	.27	.19	.01	−.12	.00	−.15	−.30	.22	−.08
69.	−.11	.16	.14	.21	.18	−.01	.23	−.31	.11	.29
70.	−.06	.44	.10	−.15	.14	.25	.32	.30	.19	.15
† 73.	−.34	.29	.23	.10	−.16	.15	.12	.02	.05	.31
74.	.07	.36	.06	.26	−.09	.39	−.06	−.07	−.09	−.01
75.	−.00	.30	.03	.22	.04	.04	.02	−.09	.52	.19
77.	.30	.38	−.08	−.17	−.26	.11	.19	−.22	−.10	.11
78.	.07	−.24	−.02	−.18	−.15	.25	.18	−.13	−.23	.17
79.	.49	.13	−.07	−.03	.20	.08	.22	−.03	−.01	−.17
† 82.	.24	.16	−.27	.31	−.06	.25	.11	.02	−.26	.02
84.	−.07	.17	.20	.15	−.18	−.20	.30	.20	.03	−.06
86.	.41	−.23	.35	.20	−.18	.02	−.02	−.12	.08	.11
87.	.08	−.31	.19	.18	.06	−.06	.00	−.17	−.03	.41
88.	−.06	.65	.03	−.24	.02	.23	.19	.29	.16	−.11
89.	.31	−.05	.20	−.42	−.25	.08	.23	−.10	.15	−.09
91.	.50	−.31	.20	.02	.15	.12	−.02	.15	.22	.14
92.	.14	.24	.25	.07	.06	−.32	.41	−.20	−.08	.09

11	12	13	14	15	16	17	18	19	20	COMMU-NALITY
.30	−.09	−.01	−.22	−.17	−.01	.12	.16	.10	−.06	.61
−.27	−.13	−.22	.19	−.15	.13	−.05	.06	−.10	−.07	.54
.03	.13	−.07	−.05	.07	.11	.09	−.05	.17	−.06	.62
.04	−.05	.15	.18	.12	.21	−.17	.12	.03	.19	.69
.10	−.18	−.09	.23	−.15	.20	.18	.06	.21	.05	.65
−.27	.40	−.11	.15	−.25	−.03	.10	−.08	−.21	−.03	.68
.17	−.17	.31	.14	−.11	−.21	−.02	−.08	−.08	−.15	.67
−.11	−.03	.25	.03	−.20	.01	−.12	.13	−.01	−.12	.73
−.36	.09	.27	.09	−.05	−.13	.05	.20	.19	.01	.64
−.03	.29	−.21	−.05	.13	.30	−.25	.05	.09	.08	.67
.05	.22	−.14	.12	.19	−.19	.10	.09	.07	−.11	.69
−.15	−.02	.00	−.10	.18	.17	.14	.02	.12	−.11	.66
.11	.15	−.18	−.02	.22	.05	−.16	−.01	.04	−.01	.69
−.09	−.17	.10	−.17	−.11	−.09	−.09	.19	.25	.01	.65
.06	.21	.11	.07	.08	−.03	.13	.16	.09	.19	.63
−.02	.04	.38	−.18	.31	−.13	.02	.01	.02	.09	.54
−.10	.09	−.19	−.09	.26	−.10	.02	−.07	−.03	−.09	.67
−.16	−.13	−.11	.03	−.01	−.18	−.13	.09	−.17	.27	.68
−.04	.26	−.16	−.20	.11	−.25	.15	.01	.04	.00	.56
−.06	−.09	.10	.22	.05	−.06	.05	.20	−.03	.08	.63
−.26	−.09	.23	−.11	.13	.15	.27	−.24	−.13	−.28	.66
.00	−.11	−.07	−.14	.09	−.09	−.03	.01	−.05	.02	.51
−.03	−.16	−.01	.33	.05	−.10	.23	−.12	−.16	.07	.69
.05	.18	.21	.08	−.05	.19	.26	.01	.08	−.11	.59
−.28	−.01	.14	−.10	.16	.18	.05	.06	.19	.24	.65
−.06	−.03	−.10	−.04	.00	−.09	−.03	−.22	.17	.04	.66
−.20	.02	−.00	−.23	.20	.09	−.12	.29	−.08	−.25	.73
−.15	−.18	−.21	−.04	.03	−.03	.22	−.05	−.03	.05	.54
.16	−.16	−.13	.05	.17	−.14	−.01	.02	−.12	−.10	.61
−.13	.22	.15	.02	−.03	.21	−.17	−.05	−.24	.12	.69
.32	.17	.17	.13	−.12	.17	.28	.11	.07	.03	.63
.22	−.04	−.07	−.13	−.05	.16	−.17	.08	−.30	−.08	.62
.19	−.22	−.04	.22	−.07	.06	−.17	−.13	.16	−.22	.65
.36	.29	−.08	.10	−.07	.13	.08	.24	.11	.01	.63
.21	.07	.07	−.28	−.26	−.14	.02	−.09	.03	−.09	.69
.06	.05	.23	−.05	−.02	.02	−.45	−.19	.09	−.02	.68
.04	.08	.06	.04	.07	−.11	.01	−.20	.13	.06	.78
.06	−.11	.18	−.06	−.01	−.07	.03	.28	−.06	.12	.63
.08	.17	−.08	−.11	−.00	−.12	.14	−.06	−.11	−.00	.62
.15	−.17	−.22	−.28	.10	.13	.07	−.01	.11	−.01	.70

ITEM	1	2	3	4	5	6	7	8	9	10
93.	.04	.26	.13	.30	.25	.03	−.06	.22	−.36	−.10
94.	.36	.01	−.13	.18	−.12	.23	.04	.03	−.19	.11
† 95.	.25	.14	.34	−.10	−.26	.08	−.36	.27	−.20	.11
96.	.34	.27	.42	−.17	−.20	.05	−.09	.06	−.15	.05
97.	.14	.12	.37	−.02	.50	−.23	−.14	−.02	−.09	.17
99.	.19	.09	.41	.05	.06	−.40	−.07	.08	−.14	−.10
101.	.34	.24	−.17	−.08	−.16	−.11	.32	.04	−.28	.09
†102.	.20	.17	−.20	.49	−.03	.05	.06	.06	−.22	.16
103.	.18	.33	−.19	.20	.21	.02	−.28	.02	.23	.11
105.	.13	.02	.05	.12	−.07	.46	−.13	−.14	.04	−.02
106.	.04	−.25	.07	−.34	−.01	.27	.08	.11	.10	−.29
107.	.15	−.22	.39	−.20	.35	.17	.13	−.17	−.05	−.12
108.	.14	.10	.45	.20	−.18	−.27	−.13	−.08	−.03	−.27
109.	.38	−.14	.48	.22	−.15	.18	−.08	−.12	.01	−.07
Eigen Value	4.85	3.30	2.46	2.31	2.03	1.92	1.74	1.73	1.50	1.45
Proportion of Variation	.09	.06	.05	.04	.04	.04	.03	.03	.03	.03
Cumulative Proportion	.09	.15	.20	.24	.28	.31	.34	.38	.40	.43

†Reversed Items

11	12	13	14	15	16	17	18	19	20	COMMU-NALITY
.01	−.02	.22	−.12	.05	−.14	.02	.21	−.22	.02	.61
.31	−.14	.05	−.02	.31	.16	−.00	.05	−.25	.21	.65
.03	−.22	.08	.19	.28	−.01	−.05	.01	.10	−.05	.71
−.01	−.07	.05	.21	.12	.07	−.01	−.03	−.03	−.39	.89
−.08	−.09	−.11	.18	.07	.06	.11	.05	−.11	.07	.63
−.16	−.28	−.14	−.05	−.15	.06	.11	−.01	.06	.27	.67
−.18	.04	−.04	.07	−.02	−.12	−.11	−.08	.34	.03	.63
.05	.12	.16	−.13	−.07	−.11	.16	−.29	−.12	.26	.71
−.02	.11	.06	.06	−.19	.24	−.15	−.21	−.14	.13	.63
.11	.00	−.19	.16	−.10	−.43	−.15	.12	−.00	.09	.60
.09	−.25	−.01	−.19	−.01	.18	.11	−.22	.07	.22	.62
.06	.19	−.03	.24	.16	−.02	−.08	−.07	.11	.15	.65
.17	.00	.18	.08	.17	−.15	−.09	−.25	.12	.05	.69
−.08	−.07	−.01	−.23	−.31	.03	−.09	.04	.09	−.00	.71
3.40	1.34	1.27	1.23	1.20	1.17	1.10	1.04	1.02	1.01	
.03	.02	.02	.02	.02	.02	.02	.02	.02	.02	
.46	.48	.51	.53	.55	.57	.59	.61	.63	.65	

APPENDIX
·*D*·

Fisher/Tack Effective Leadership Inventory

Directions: This questionnaire is designed to identify the characteristics of an effective college president (chancellor) and focuses on the following three areas: styles/attitudes, professional information, and personal data. Please provide the information in the format requested.

PART I: PERSONAL ATTITUDES AND LEADERSHIP STYLE

Please react to the following statements about your own characteristics as a leader by checking the appropriate responses. Your responses should represent your perceptions of yourself as a leader.

SA = Strongly Agree   A = Agree   UD = Undecided
D = Disagree   SD = Strongly Disagree

As a college president, I:

	SA	A	UD	D	SD
1. Am sometimes viewed as hard-nosed.	[ ]	[ ]	[ ]	[ ]	[ ]
2. Believe that the respect of those to be led is essential.	[ ]	[ ]	[ ]	[ ]	[ ]
3. Believe that an effective leader takes risks.	[ ]	[ ]	[ ]	[ ]	[ ]
4. Am primarily concerned about being liked.	[ ]	[ ]	[ ]	[ ]	[ ]
5. Try to achieve consensus.	[ ]	[ ]	[ ]	[ ]	[ ]
6. Believe in organizational structure.	[ ]	[ ]	[ ]	[ ]	[ ]
7. Believe that the leader should be perceived as self-confident.	[ ]	[ ]	[ ]	[ ]	[ ]
8. Belief in close collegial relationships.	[ ]	[ ]	[ ]	[ ]	[ ]
9. Believe that a leader serves the people.	[ ]	[ ]	[ ]	[ ]	[ ]
10. Believe in merit pay.	[ ]	[ ]	[ ]	[ ]	[ ]
11. Am sometimes viewed as assertive.	[ ]	[ ]	[ ]	[ ]	[ ]
12. Am rarely in keeping with the status quo.	[ ]	[ ]	[ ]	[ ]	[ ]
13. Delegate responsibility and authority to subordinates.	[ ]	[ ]	[ ]	[ ]	[ ]
14. Believe in the value of one-on-one meetings.	[ ]	[ ]	[ ]	[ ]	[ ]
15. Maintain a measure of mystique.	[ ]	[ ]	[ ]	[ ]	[ ]
16. Use large social functions to advance the institution.	[ ]	[ ]	[ ]	[ ]	[ ]
17. Choose another CEO as a confidant.	[ ]	[ ]	[ ]	[ ]	[ ]
18. Believe in community involvement.	[ ]	[ ]	[ ]	[ ]	[ ]
19. Always appear energetic.	[ ]	[ ]	[ ]	[ ]	[ ]
20. Am often viewed as a loner.	[ ]	[ ]	[ ]	[ ]	[ ]

As a college president, I:

	SA	A	UD	D	SD
21. Count committee meetings as mistakes.	[ ]	[ ]	[ ]	[ ]	[ ]
22. Would rather be viewed as a strong leader than a good colleague.	[ ]	[ ]	[ ]	[ ]	[ ]
23. Accept losses gracefully.	[ ]	[ ]	[ ]	[ ]	[ ]
24. Tend to work long hours.	[ ]	[ ]	[ ]	[ ]	[ ]
25. Often like people who are different.	[ ]	[ ]	[ ]	[ ]	[ ]
26. Only occasionally speak spontaneously.	[ ]	[ ]	[ ]	[ ]	[ ]
27. Am warm and affable.	[ ]	[ ]	'[ ]	[ ]	[ ]
28. Would rather be influential than professionally admired.	[ ]	[ ]	[ ]	[ ]	[ ]
29. Dress well.	[ ]	[ ]	[ ]	[ ]	[ ]
30. Deeply care about the welfare of the individual.	[ ]	[ ]	[ ]	[ ]	[ ]
31. Believe in the institution at all costs.	[ ]	[ ]	[ ]	[ ]	[ ]
32. Encourage creative types even though often in disagreement.	[ ]	[ ]	[ ]	[ ]	[ ]
33. Appear to make decisions easily.	[ ]	[ ]	[ ]	[ ]	[ ]
34. Appear confident even when in doubt.	[ ]	[ ]	[ ]	[ ]	[ ]
35. View myself and the institution as one.	[ ]	[ ]	[ ]	[ ]	[ ]
36. Am often seen as somewhat aloof.	[ ]	[ ]	[ ]	[ ]	[ ]
37. Enjoy stirring things up.	[ ]	[ ]	[ ]	[ ]	[ ]
38. Am rarely viewed as flamboyant.	[ ]	[ ]	[ ]	[ ]	[ ]
39. Appear to enjoy the perquisites of office.	[ ]	[ ]	[ ]	[ ]	[ ]
40. Smile a lot.	[ ]	[ ]	[ ]	[ ]	[ ]

PART II: PROFESSIONAL DATA

Degrees Earned

Doctorate:

        No   [ ]
        Yes [ ]

        If yes, type of degree:
        PhD [ ] DFA [ ] JD   [ ] Other (specify) [ ]
        EdD [ ] DBA [ ] MD [ ] _____

        Institution granting degree: _____
        Type of institution: Public   [ ]
                           Private [ ]

        Major: _____

Master's:

        No   [ ]
        Yes [ ]

        If yes, type of degree:
        MA   [ ] MBA [ ] Other (specify) [ ]
        MEd [ ] MFA [ ] _____

        Institution granting degree: _____
        Type of institution: Public   [ ]
                           Private [ ]

        Major: _____

Baccalaureate:

        No   [ ]
        Yes [ ]

        If yes, type of degree:
        BS [ ] BFA [ ]
        BA [ ] Other (specify) [ ]

_____

Institution granting degree: _____

Type of institution: Public   [   ]

                Private   [   ]

Major: _____

Previous Experience

Positions held in higher education (beginning with the first position, indicate the offices you have held using the codes listed below. When designating associate or assistant positions, codes should be combined, e.g., JE = assistant dean. If you changed institutions but kept the same title, please make separate entries for each position occupied. Additionally, please refer to the institutional codes when identifying the type of institution at which you were employed.)

POSITION CODES		INSTITUTIONAL CODES
A = Full-time faculty member	F = Assistant-to-the	1 = 4-year, public
B = Department chairperson	G = Vice President	2 = 4-year, private
C = Coordinator	H = President	3 = 2-year, public
D = Director	I = Associate	4 = 2-year, private
E = Dean	J = Assistant	
	K = Other	

POSITION CHRONOLOGY	POSITION CODE	AREA	YEARS IN POSITION	TYPE OF INSTITUTION
1	_____	_____	_____	_____
2	_____	_____	_____	_____
3	_____	_____	_____	_____
4	_____	_____	_____	_____
5	_____	_____	_____	_____
6	_____	_____	_____	_____
7	_____	_____	_____	_____
8	_____	_____	_____	_____
9	_____	_____	_____	_____

POSITION CHRONOLOGY	POSITION CODE	AREA	YEARS IN POSITION	TYPE OF INSTITUTION
10	_____	_____	_____	_____
11	_____	_____	_____	_____
12	_____	_____	_____	_____

Total years in higher
education administration: _____

Total years in presidential
position: _____

Total years of experience
outside higher education: _____

Age upon assumption of
first presidency: _____

Current Position

Years in current presidency: _____

Type of institution: Public [ ]   Two-year [ ]
                     Private [ ]   Four-year [ ]

Student population (head count)   Salary: _____
of campus: _____

Scholarly Activity

Number of books published: _____
Approximate number of articles in refereed journals: _____
Approximate number of professional organization
memberships: _____
Two professional organizations in which you participate
frequently:
        Organization #1: _____
        Office(s) Held: _____
        Organization #2: _____
        Office(s) Held: _____

PART III: PERSONAL INFORMATION

Age: ____   Sex: Male   [ ]
                         Female [ ]

Race: American Indian [ ]   Filipino [ ]
     Asian Indian [ ]   Japanese [ ]
     Black [ ]   Spanish/Hispanic [ ]
     Caucasian [ ]   Other (specify) [ ]
     Chinese [ ]

Religious Preference:
    Eastern Orthodox [ ]   Baptist [ ]
    Jewish [ ]   Episcopal [ ]
    Muslim [ ]   Methodist [ ]
    Roman Catholic [ ]   Presbyterian [ ]
    Protestant [ ]   Other (specify) [ ]

Marital status: Number of marriages:
    Never married [ ]   0 [ ]
    Divorced [ ]   1 [ ]
    Widowed [ ]   2 [ ]
    Now married [ ]   3 [ ]
              4 [ ]

Spouse's Occupation: (check one)
    Professional (e.g., accountant, engineer, lawyer, doctor, etc.) [ ]
    Manager, business official (e.g., finance manager, sales administrator, etc.) [ ]
    Proprietor or business owner (e.g., contractor, gasoline dealership, etc.) [ ]
    Sales and clerical (e.g., billing clerk, mail carrier, insurance sales, etc.) [ ]
    Technician/semiprofessional (e.g., draftsperson, surveyor, health therapy, etc.) [ ]
    Craftsman or foreman (e.g., carpenter, jeweler, mechanic, etc.) [ ]
    Skilled machine operator (e.g., drill press, lathe, truck driver, etc.) [ ]
    Service worker (e.g., police officer, hospital orderly, barber, etc.) [ ]

Laborer (e.g., construction, factory, gas station, etc.)   [ ]
Farmer   [ ]
Other (specify)   [ ]

Number of children: 0   [ ]   Ages of children: _____
                       1   [ ]   _____
                       2   [ ]   _____
                       3   [ ]   _____
                       4   [ ]   _____
                       5+   [ ]   _____

State or foreign country   Political Affiliation:
of birth: _____   American Independent[ ]
State of current   Democrat   [ ]
residence: _____   Republican   [ ]
                                   Other (specify)   [ ]

Father's education:

Less than high school   [ ]   Post-baccalaureate courses   [ ]
Some high school   [ ]   Master's degree   [ ]
High school diploma   [ ]   Doctoral degree   [ ]
College courses   [ ]   Post-doctoral work   [ ]
Baccalaureate degree   [ ]

Mother's education:

Less than high school   [ ]   Post-baccalaureate courses[ ]
Some high school   [ ]   Master's degree   [ ]
High school diploma   [ ]   Doctoral degree   [ ]
College courses   [ ]   Post-doctoral work   [ ]
Baccalaureate degree   [ ]

Number of siblings:

Younger brothers   _____   Older brothers   _____
Younger sisters   _____   Older sisters   _____

Please return this instrument to:
    Bowling Green State University
    ATTN: Dr. Martha W. Tack, EDAS
    Bowling Green, OH 43403

APPENDIX
·E·

Cover Letter

December 2, 1985

Dear

Never before in the history of postsecondary education has there been such an obvious need for strong leadership at the presidential level. Although the presidency has been the focal point of a number of recent studies, we still do not have sufficient information about the factors that enhance a chief executive officer's effectiveness. Consequently, James L. Fisher and I, with the support of the Exxon Education Foundation, are conducting a nationwide study designed to identify the characteristics of an effective college president or chancellor.

Because of your commitment to effectiveness and efficiency at your institution and your knowledge of the presidency, we ask now that you complete the attached survey instrument and return it in the enclosed envelope by December 13, 1985. In order to

151

assure the anonymity of your responses, several safeguards have been developed. As you will notice, a code number is included on the prepaid response envelope. I assigned this code number for follow-up purposes and have the list of names and codes under lock and key. I will maintain the list until the survey process is complete; then the list will be destroyed so that neither your name nor the name of your institution will ever be associated with your responses.

The research project is being conducted in three phases. Phase I involved the identification of individuals who, in the eyes of their peers and associates, are effective college presidents or chancellors. Phase II focuses on the collection of data using the attached instrument that was pilot tested with 265 college/university presidents. During Phase III, project staff members will interview selected college presidents and chancellors to obtain additional information about the factors that enhance a chief executive officer's effectiveness.

If you have any questions, please contact either Jim Fisher at 202-328-5925 or me at 419-372-7283. We certainly hope you will participate in this effort to learn more about the presidency and look forward to sharing the research results with you in the future.

Most cordially,

Martha W. Tack, PhD
Professor and Coordinator of Graduate Studies in EDAS

Attachments

The Effective College President: Interview Guide

PRESIDENTIAL ROLE/IMAGE MANAGEMENT

What do you believe the role of a president to be?

What image do you strive to create?
Is this image projected differently based on the situation and/or the constituency with whom you are working? If so, how?

How do you conduct yourself with external groups (both policy and practice)?
Media?
Alumni?
Legislators?
Business/Industrial leaders?
General public?
Politicians?

How do you conduct yourself with internal constituents?
Faculty?
Staff?
Students?

Do you believe faculty, staff, and students have an important role to play in governance?
> If so, how do you involve them in governance?
> If not, why not?

Do faculty, staff, and students have direct access to you? If so, how?
What are the qualities you seek in your key staff?

How many scheduled public appearances do you make generally each week with medium-to-large sized groups?
> What types of groups are involved?

RELATIONSHIP WITH BOARD OF TRUSTEES

How do you view the role of the board of trustees?

What type of relationship do you have with your board of trustees?
> If these items are not mentioned, ask about them:
>> How frequently do you interact with board members?
>> How do you keep the board focused on policy development rather than implementation?
>> Do you cultivate the friendship of board members?
>> Are you open with the board about personal issues?
>> What types of social contacts do you have with board members?

PERSONAL RELATIONSHIPS AND LEISURE TIME

Is there value in distance between you and your subordinates?
> If so, why?
> If not, why not?
> If these areas are not mentioned, ask about them:
>> Key staff
>> Deans
>> Faculty

Do you have a confidant?
> If so, why did you select him/her?
> If not, why not?

What do you believe the role of a mentor to be?
>   Did or do you have a mentor?
>   What are the most important things he/she taught you?
>   How many people have you mentored?
>   Do you currently serve as a mentor?
>   Why did you select this particular individual?

What produces tension in your life and how do you reduce it?
How do you vacation and how frequently?
What do you read?
Who are your heroes/heroines?
What are your personal and professional goals?

Have you been successful in your personal life?
>   If not, why not?
>   If so, how so?

If you have a spouse, what is his/her role in your presidency?

PRESIDENTIAL PROFILE

Would you summarize the personal and professional characteristics that contribute to your effectiveness as a college or university president?
>   If these items are not mentioned, ask about them:
>   >   How would you describe your personality and how do you use these traits to your advantage?
>   >   Which one of your academic credentials is the most important?
>   >   What early leadership experiences did you have (paid or unpaid) that made you aware of your leadership skills?
>   >   What professional experiences have you had that contributed to your effectiveness?

How do you describe your leadership style?
>   If these items are not mentioned, ask about them:
>   >   Describe your human relations skills.
>   >   Is visibility important to you?
>   If yes, why?
>   If not, why not?
Are you philosophical by nature? If so, in what ways?

Do you consider yourself a dreamer, a visionary?
If yes, why?
If not, why not?
On what is your power based?

What personal values guide your decisions and actions?

What prohibits your effectiveness and how do you overcome these obstacles?

What is the greatest professional mistake you have ever made and what did you learn from it?

If you were asked to develop a curriculum for the preparation of aspiring college presidents, what would you include in it?

What motivated you to become a president and what keeps you going now?

What would you have done if you had not become a college president?

What is the most positive thing people can say about you?

Are there any comments that you would like to make about the effectiveness of a college president?

APPENDIX ·G·

Statistical Methodology

HYPOTHESES

The following null hypotheses were used to study personal attitudes, leadership style, and demographic profiles of college presidents:

H_1 There is no significant difference between the responses of effective and representative presidents regarding management style, human relations, confidence, social reference, and the image of the president.

   H_{1a} There is no significant difference between and among the responses of effective presidents nominated one, two, and three or more times; interviewed presidents; and representative presidents.

H_2 There is no significant difference between effective and representative presidents regarding professional credentials and experiences, scholarly activities, and personal profiles.

157

THE INSTRUMENT

The instrument used to gather data is a self-report inventory with three main sections. Part I is a series of statements (Items 1–40) to which respondents are asked to indicate their perceptions of themselves as leaders. We use a 5-point Likert scale where 1 equals "Strongly Agree" and 5 equals "Strongly Disagree," except for nine items where the point values for each response were reversed, so that 5 equals "Strongly Agree" and 1 equals "Strongly Disagree." Furthermore, to ensure a maximum number of usable returned responses, unanswered questions were assigned the value of 3, which was designated "Undecided." Part II comprises a series of questions designed to elicit professional data, including detailed information related to degrees earned, previous experience, current position, and scholarly activity. Personal demographic data were collected in Part III. This information includes age, sex, race, religious preference, marital and familial data, political affiliation, place of birth and current residence, and parents' education.

STATISTICAL ANALYSIS

Data were processed using the SAS software system (SAS Institute Inc., 1985). Appropriate statistical methods were determined by classifying data according to type and number of groups to be compared.

We obtained descriptive statistics for all variables from a frequency distribution. Results were presented as absolute frequencies and adjusted percentages. Additionally, mean scores were calculated for Part I and items assigned numerical values in Part II and Part III of the Inventory.

We used analysis of variance (ANOVA), t-tests, and chi-square statistics to examine the relationship between variables. ANOVA was used to determine differences between personal attitudes and leadership style when three or more groups were under consideration. When the overall F ratios were significant, Scheffe's S method was used to make all possible comparisons among means.

T-tests were performed to determine differences in mean scores on the descriptiveness of personal attitudes and leadership style questions when two groups were under consideration. Chi-square was used to determine significant differences between groups on all demographic questions. For ANOVA, t-tests, and chi-square, significance was calculated at the .05 probability level.

APPENDIX
·H·

Frequency of Response to Demographic Items

Item	Total	Effective N	%	Representative N	%	df	X^2	p
Degrees								
Doctorate	534	280	89.74	254	83.83	3	7.03	.07
PhD		194	62.18	163	53.80			
EdD		63	20.19	75	24.75			
Theology/Religion		5	1.60	8	2.64			
Other		18	5.77	8	2.64			
Master's	523	256	82.05	267	88.11	5	6.40	.27
MA		153	49.04	135	44.55			
MEd		42	13.46	56	18.48			
MBA		7	2.24	14	4.62			
MS		32	10.26	33	10.89			
Theology/Religion		12	3.85	14	4.62			
Other		10	3.21	15	4.95			

*$p < .05$
**$p < .01$
***$p < .001$
****$p < .0001$

Item	TOTAL	EFFECTIVE		REPRESENTATIVE		df	X^2	p
		N	%	N	%			
Baccalaureate	577	294	94.23	283	93.40	2	4.91	.09
BS		101	32.37	122	40.26			
BA		179	57.37	147	48.51			
Other		14	4.49	14	4.62			
Institutions								
Doctorate	532	278	89.10	254	83.83	1	15.83	.0001****
Public		141	45.19	172	56.77			
Private		137	43.91	82	27.06			
Master's	530	259	83.01	271	89.44	1	5.67	.02*
Public		137	43.91	171	56.44			
Private		122	39.10	100	33.00			
Baccalaureate	579	292	93.59	287	94.72	1	1.05	.31
Public		127	40.71	137	45.21			
Private		165	52.88	150	49.50			
Majors								
Doctorate	524	275	88.14	249	82.18	9	13.38	.15
Education		112	35.90	131	43.23			
Engineering		7	2.24	6	1.98			
Letters		15	4.81	16	5.28			
Life Science		11	3.53	9	2.97			
Physical Science		10	3.21	11	3.63			
Psychology		8	2.56	6	1.98			
Social Science		59	18.91	28	9.24			
Philosophy/ Religion		21	6.73	17	5.61			
Combination of majors		12	3.85	8	2.64			
Other		20	6.41	17	5.61			
Master's	508	246	78.85	262	86.47	11	16.13	.14
Business		5	1.60	13	4.29			
Education		78	25.00	98	32.34			
Engineering		7	2.24	6	1.98			
Letters		23	7.37	30	9.90			
Life Science		8	2.56	12	3.96			
Mathematics		9	2.88	6	1.98			
Physical Science		9	2.88	11	3.63			
Psychology		5	1.60	10	3.30			
Social Science		52	16.67	37	12.21			
Philosophy/ Religion		17	5.45	19	6.27			
Combination of majors		21	6.73	15	4.95			
Other		12	3.85	5	1.65			
Baccalaureate	573	290	92.95	283	93.40	11	30.63	.001***
Business		7	2.24	21	6.93			

Item	Total	Effective		Representative		df	X^2	p
		N	%	N	%			
Education		36	11.54	57	18.81			
Engineering		7	2.24	17	5.61			
Letters		34	10.90	33	10.89			
Life Science		14	4.49	17	5.61			
Mathematics		13	4.17	5	1.66			
Physical Science		13	4.17	16	5.28			
Psychology		7	2.24	8	2.64			
Social Science		82	26.28	51	16.83			
Philosophy/ Religion		14	4.49	13	4.29			
Combination of majors		53	16.99	36	11.88			
Other		10	3.21	9	2.97			
Career Path								
Beginning position	551	284	91.03	267	88.12	8	5.57	.70
Faculty		187	59.93	165	54.46			
Chair		6	1.92	9	2.97			
Assistant/ Associate Director		6	1.92	5	1.65			
Assistant/ Associate Dean		10	3.20	6	1.98			
Director		22	7.05	27	8.91			
Dean		16	5.12	12	3.96			
Assistant to the President		7	2.24	5	1.65			
Other administration		12	3.84	19	6.27			
Other		18	5.76	19	6.27			
Beginning Area	469	234	75.00	235	77.56	4	2.33	.68
Academic Affairs		10	3.20	6	1.98			
Student Affairs		31	9.93	32	10.56			
External Affairs		7	2.24	11	3.63			
Instruction		167	53.52	163	53.79			
Other		19	6.08	23	7.59			
Years in Beginning Position	554	287	91.99	267	88.12	2	0.42	.81
1–3 years		165	52.88	147	48.51			
4–10 years		101	32.37	101	33.33			
Over 10 years		21	6.73	19	6.27			
Beginning Institution Type	539	282	90.38	257	84.82	3	3.00	.39
4-year public		93	29.80	88	29.04			
4-year private		125	40.06	97	32.01			
2-year public		52	16.66	58	19.14			
2-year private		12	3.84	14	4.62			

Item	TOTAL	EFFECTIVE		REPRESENTATIVE		df	X^2	p
		N	%	N	%			
Last position prior								
to presidency	545	280	89.42	264	87.12	7	7.48	.38
Vice President		130	41.66	123	40.59			
Dean		85	27.24	75	24.75			
Director		10	3.20	21	6.93			
Chair		5	1.60	6	1.98			
Faculty		9	2.88	11	3.63			
Assistant to the								
President		13	4.16	12	3.96			
Assistant/								
Associate								
Administrator		9	2.88	5	1.65			
Other		18	5.76	11	3.63			
Last Area Prior to								
Presidency	392	185	59.29	207	68.32	5	3.15	.68
Academic Affairs		74	23.72	75	24.75			
External Affairs		12	3.85	22	7.26			
General								
Administration		32	10.26	33	10.89			
Instruction		31	9.94	35	11.55			
Student Affairs		18	5.77	17	5.61			
Other		18	5.77	25	8.25			
Years in last position								
prior to								
presidency	546	280	89.74	266	87.79	2	4.98	.08
1–3 years		135	43.27	113	37.29			
4–10 years		132	42.30	147	48.51			
Over 10 years		13	4.17	6	1.98			
Last institution type								
prior to								
presidency	530	270	86.54	260	85.81	3	13.47	.004**
4-year public		100	32.05	68	22.44			
4-year private		102	32.69	90	29.70			
2-year public		61	19.55	91	30.03			
2-year private		7	2.24	11	3.63			
Age of assumption								
of presidency	592	301	96.47	291	96.04	2	6.22	.05*
Over 49		31	9.93	47	15.51			
40–49		165	52.88	163	53.79			
Under 40		105	33.65	81	26.73			
Years of higher								
education								
administration	602	309	99.04	293	96.70	4	7.88	.10
1–10		27	8.65	41	13.53			
11–15		56	17.95	58	19.14			
16–20		89	28.53	89	29.37			

Item	Total	Effective N	Effective %	Representative N	Representative %	df	X^2	p
21–25		74	23.72	64	21.12			
Over 25		63	20.19	41	13.53			
Years outside higher education	601	304	97.44	296	97.69	2	50.98	.0001****
1–4		32	10.26	102	33.66			
5–10		133	42.63	106	34.98			
Over 10		139	44.55	88	29.04			
Years in current presidency	595	299	95.83	295	97.36	2	30.92	.0001****
1–4		67	21.47	129	42.57			
5–10		131	41.99	99	32.67			
Over 10		101	32.37	67	22.11			
Type of current institution	615	312	100.00	303	100.00	3	18.40	.0001****
4-year public		92	29.49	68	22.44			
4-year private		129	41.35	106	34.98			
2-year public		88	28.20	112	36.96			
2-year private		3	.97	17	5.61			
Years in presidential position	436	221	70.83	215	70.96	3	2.12	.55
0		6	1.92	6	1.98			
1–4		82	26.28	71	23.43			
5–10		88	28.20	82	27.06			
Over 10		45	14.42	56	18.48			
Head count	607	308	98.72	299	98.68	7	54.37	.0001****
1–1,000		23	7.37	74	24.42			
1,001–2,500		80	25.64	80	26.40			
2,501–5,000		57	18.27	59	19.47			
5,001–10,000		57	18.27	44	14.52			
10,001–15,000		28	8.97	19	6.27			
15,001–20,000		14	4.49	12	3.96			
20,001–30,000		24	7.69	5	1.65			
Over 30,000		25	8.01	6	1.98			
Salary	555	283	90.71	272	89.77	6	74.97	.0001****
Under $40,000		3	.96	21	6.93			
$40,001–50,000		9	2.89	28	9.24			
$50,001–60,000		36	11.54	65	21.45			
$60,001–75,000		85	27.24	101	33.33			
$75,001–100,000		117	37.50	47	15.51			
$100,001– 125,000		24	7.69	7	2.31			
Over $125,000		9	2.89	3	.99			
Published articles	531	268	85.90	263	86.79	5	16.86	.005**
0		46	14.74	56	18.48			
1–5		83	26.60	113	37.29			

	TOTAL	EFFECTIVE		REPRESENTATIVE				
Item		N	%	N	%	df	X^2	p
6–10		57	18.27	40	13.20			
11–15		20	6.41	20	6.60			
16–20		21	6.73	10	3.30			
Over 20		41	13.14	24	7.92			
Published books	478	249	79.81	229	75.58	5	18.86	.001***
Zero		118	37.82	148	48.84			
One		48	15.38	42	13.86			
Two		40	12.82	19	6.27			
Three		20	6.41	9	2.97			
Over Three		23	7.37	11	3.63			
Number of professional organizations	529	264	84.62	265	87.46	3	8.73	.03*
1–3		42	13.46	51	16.83			
4–6		123	39.42	146	48.18			
7–10		64	20.51	42	13.86			
Over 10		35	11.21	26	8.58			
Names of professional organizations								
First organization listed	504	259	83.01	245	80.86	8	21.47	.006**
American Association of Community and Junior Colleges		36	11.54	29	9.57			
American Association of State Colleges and Universities		30	9.62	29	9.57			
American Council on Education		22	7.05	11	3.63			
National Association of Independent Colleges and Universities		10	3.20	9	2.97			
National		41	13.14	50	16.50			
Other National Higher Education Emphasis		28	8.97	11	3.63			
Regional		6	1.92	15	4.95			
State		30	9.62	47	15.51			
Other		56	17.95	44	14.52			

Item	Total	Effective		Representative		df	X^2	p
		N	%	N	%			
Second organization listed	445	231	74.04	214	70.63	7	25.75	.001***
American Association of Community and Junior Colleges		15	4.80	11	3.63			
American Association of State Colleges and Universities		7	2.24	5	1.65			
American Council on Education		30	9.62	10	3.30			
National		33	10.58	49	16.17			
Other National Higher Education Emphasis		40	12.82	18	5.94			
Regional		21	6.73	19	6.27			
State		38	12.18	57	18.81			
Other		47	15.06	45	14.85			
Organizational offices								
Office held in first organization	315	196	62.82	119	39.27	5	9.33	.10
Board of Directors		53	16.99	21	6.93			
President		25	8.01	20	6.60			
Vice President		10	3.20	7	2.31			
Committee Chair		48	15.38	21	6.93			
Committee member		42	13.46	30	9.90			
Other		18	5.77	20	6.60			
Office held in second organization	277	160	51.28	117	38.61	5	5.06	.41
Board of Directors		31	9.93	17	5.61			
President		34	10.90	28	9.24			
Vice President		7	2.24	7	2.31			
Committee Chair		32	10.26	20	6.60			
Committee member		37	11.86	22	7.26			
Other		19	6.08	23	7.59			
Current age	536	266	85.26	270	89.11	2	15.50	.0001****
Over 59		52	16.67	52	17.16			
50–59		145	46.47	107	35.31			
Under 50		69	22.11	111	36.63			

Item	TOTAL	EFFECTIVE		REPRESENTATIVE		df	X²	p
		N	%	N	%			
Number of children	589	299	95.83	290	95.71	5	2.16	.83
Zero		31	9.94	24	7.92			
One		19	6.09	21	6.93			
Two		95	30.45	99	32.67			
Three		91	29.17	89	29.37			
Four		48	15.38	39	12.87			
Five		15	4.81	18	5.94			
Ages of children								
First child	511	258	82.69	253	83.50	3	12.13	.007**
Under 18		37	11.86	62	20.46			
18–22		44	14.10	53	17.49			
23–30		121	38.78	91	30.03			
Over 30		56	17.95	47	15.51			
Second child	482	242	77.56	240	79.21	3	9.58	.02*
Under 18		38	12.17	61	20.13			
18–22		51	16.35	58	19.14			
23–30		112	35.90	87	28.71			
Over 30		41	13.14	34	11.22			
Third child	294	152	48.72	142	46.86	3	9.05	.03*
Under 18		31	9.94	48	15.84			
18–22		51	16.35	30	9.90			
23–30		54	17.31	49	16.17			
Over 30		16	5.13	15	4.95			
Fourth child	114	59	18.91	55	18.15	2	0.59	.74
Under 18		18	5.77	15	4.95			
18–22		13	4.17	10	3.30			
Over 22		28	8.97	30	9.90			
Fifth child	35	18	5.77	17	5.61	1	1.45	.23
Under 23		10	3.21	6	1.98			
Over 22		8	2.56	11	3.63			
Sex	611	309	99.04	302	99.67	1	0.19	.66
Male		276	88.46	273	90.10			
Female		33	10.58	29	9.58			
Race	588	299	95.83	289	95.38	2	2.01	.37
Black		16	5.13	12	3.96			
Caucasian		276	88.46	274	90.43			
Other		7	2.24	3	1.00			
Religious preference	589	302	96.79	287	94.72	3	4.35	.23
Jewish		15	4.80	12	3.96			
Protestant		226	72.44	197	65.01			
Roman Catholic		53	16.99	65	21.45			
Other		8	2.56	13	4.29			

Item	Total	Effective		Representative		df	X^2	p
		N	%	N	%			
Birthplace area	539	275	88.14	264	87.13	5	2.59	.76
Middle States Association of Colleges and Schools		69	22.12	54	17.82			
New England Association of Schools and Colleges		15	4.81	19	6.27			
North Central Association of Colleges and Schools		106	33.97	112	39.96			
Northwest Association of Schools and Colleges		10	3.20	10	3.30			
Southern Association of Colleges and Schools		65	20.83	61	20.13			
Western Association of Schools and Colleges		10	3.20	8	2.64			
Current residence area	615	312	100.00	303	100.00	5	3.10	.68
Middle States Association of Colleges and Schools		58	18.58	46	15.18			
New England Association of Schools and Colleges		25	8.01	18	5.94			
North Central Association of Colleges and Schools		103	33.01	106	34.98			
Northwest Association of Schools and Colleges		17	5.45	19	6.27			
Southern Association of Colleges and Schools		89	28.53	89	29.37			

Item	Total	Effective		Representative		df	X^2	p
		N	%	N	%			
Western Association of Schools and Colleges		20	6.41	25	8.25			
Birth position	530	266	85.26	264	87.13	3	1.02	.80
Only child		31	9.93	27	8.91			
First child		101	32.37	103	33.99			
Second child		68	21.79	61	20.13			
Third or higher		66	21.15	73	24.09			
Marital status	600	299	95.83	294	97.03	2	1.99	.37
Now married		257	82.37	257	84.82			
Never married		26	8.33	28	9.24			
Divorced		16	5.13	9	2.97			
Number of marriages	579	288	92.31	282	93.07	2	0.42	.81
Zero		16	5.13	15	4.95			
One		246	78.85	137	78.22			
Two		26	8.33	30	9.90			
Spouse occupation	522	263	84.29	259	85.48	7	8.97	.26
Professional		129	41.35	119	39.27			
Manager or business official		16	5.13	16	5.28			
Proprietor or business owner		6	1.92	10	3.30			
Sales and clerical		7	2.25	14	4.62			
Homemaker		59	18.91	71	23.45			
Unpaid employee		20	6.41	13	4.29			
Musician or singer		12	3.85	6	1.98			
Other		14	4.49	10	3.30			
Political affiliation	560	282	90.38	277	91.42	3	11.50	.009**
American Independent		72	23.07	47	15.51			
Democrat		136	43.59	124	40.92			
Republican		67	21.47	97	32.01			
None		7	2.24	9	2.97			
Father's education	597	303	97.12	294	97.03	6	8.58	.20
Less than high school		125	40.06	99	32.67			
Some high school		31	9.94	33	10.89			
High school diploma		44	14.10	57	18.81			
College courses		29	9.29	43	14.19			
Baccalaureate degree		32	10.26	29	9.57			
Master's degree		25	8.01	20	6.60			
Doctoral degree		17	5.45	13	4.29			

Item	Total	Effective		Representative		df	X²	p
		N	%	N	%			
Mother's education	600	303	97.12	297	98.02	6	13.53	.04*
Less than high school		94	30.13	61	20.13			
Some high school		29	9.29	35	11.55			
High school diploma		81	25.96	95	31.35			
College courses		35	11.22	53	17.49			
Baccalaureate degree		42	13.46	34	11.22			
Post-baccalaureate courses		8	2.56	8	2.64			
Master's or higher degree		14	4.49	11	3.63			

APPENDIX
·I·

Frequency of Response to Personal Attitudes and Leadership Style Items

| | 2-YEAR | | | | | | | | | |
| | Effective (N = 91) | | | | | Representative (N = 129) | | | | |
Item	SA	A	NO	D	SD	SA	A	NO	D	SL
1. Am sometimes viewed as hard-nosed	16	55	7	13	0	19	82	10	14	4
2. Believe that the respect of those to be led is essential	70	21	0	0	0	95	31	1	2	0
3. Believe that an effective leader takes risks	63	28	0	0	0	91	37	1	0	0
† 4. Am primarily concerned about being liked	19	64	8	0	0	21	87	21	0	0
5. Try to achieve consensus	18	67	4	1	1	11	104	5	9	0
6. Believe in organizational structure	31	56	4	0	0	44	82	2	1	0
7. Believe that the leader should be perceived as self-confident	59	30	0	2	0	78	51	0	0	0
† 8. Believe in close collegial relationships	26	60	5	0	0	23	93	13	0	0
† 9. Believe that a leader serves the people	46	38	6	1	0	75	50	3	1	0
10. Believe in merit pay	18	33	28	10	2	24	64	28	11	3
11. Am sometimes viewed as assertive	30	56	2	3	0	36	79	8	6	0
†12. Am rarely in keeping with the status quo	8	34	17	32	0	16	49	25	35	4

4-YEAR									
Effective (N = 221)					Representative (N = 174)				
SA	A	NO	D	SD	SA	A	NO	D	SD
34	130	17	34	6	35	99	9	29	2
170	51	0	0	0	121	51	2	0	0
147	70	3	1	0	115	57	2	0	0
44	159	18	0	0	19	140	15	0	0
50	146	7	16	2	28	130	8	8	0
52	147	16	5	1	48	118	5	3	0
116	101	4	0	0	99	72	2	0	1
67	138	16	0	0	45	107	22	0	0
115	83	15	8	0	84	77	11	2	0
110	91	13	6	1	82	67	17	7	1
73	119	22	7	0	58	104	7	5	0
25	70	50	74	2	17	65	38	53	1

	2-Year									
	Effective (N = 91)					Representative (N = 129)				
Item	SA	A	NO	D	SD	SA	A	NO	D	SD
13. Delegate responsibility and authority to subordinates	55	36	0	0	0	73	56	0	0	0
14. Believe in the value of one-on-one meetings	42	48	1	0	0	79	48	2	0	0
15. Maintain a measure of mystique	8	36	13	28	6	11	44	25	42	7
16. Use large social functions to advance the institution	17	41	9	22	2	22	58	17	30	2
†17. Choose another CEO as a confidant	10	38	19	21	3	14	57	23	32	3
18. Believe in community involvement	60	26	4	1	0	91	34	4	0	0
19. Always appear energetic	35	48	7	1	0	42	72	9	6	0
20. Am often viewed as a loner	3	25	14	40	9	5	35	20	58	11
†21. Count committee meetings as mistakes	1	4	13	54	19	3	7	15	72	32
22. Would rather be viewed as a strong leader than a good colleague	21	40	18	12	0	27	72	20	9	1
23. Accept losses gracefully	6	50	14	21	0	6	77	15	28	3

4-YEAR									
Effective (N = 221)					Representative (N = 174)				
SA	A	NO	D	SD	SA	A	NO	D	SD
105	115	1	0	0	66	101	5	2	0
101	117	3	0	0	70	101	3	0	0
20	76	43	67	15	17	72	29	42	14
53	130	16	22	0	40	98	17	18	1
22	69	47	78	5	16	64	32	58	4
114	96	9	2	0	88	79	7	0	0
74	119	18	10	0	56	92	17	9	0
11	64	43	89	14	6	64	33	58	13
1	12	20	150	38	3	13	26	110	22
33	112	42	33	1	33	89	29	22	1
18	138	29	35	1	17	91	26	39	1

| | 2-YEAR | | | | | | | | | |
| | Effective (N = 91) | | | | | Representative (N = 129) | | | | |
Item	SA	A	NO	D	SD	SA	A	NO	D	SD
24. Tend to work long hours	33	45	6	7	0	36	76	4	13	0
†25. Often like people who are different	13	60	15	3	0	21	78	22	7	1
26. Only occasionally speak spontaneously	1	14	4	55	17	1	35	9	66	18
27. Am warm and affable	11	50	18	12	0	23	69	26	11	0
†28. Would rather be influential than professionally admired	7	18	29	36	1	8	41	27	46	7
29. Dress well	27	54	9	1	0	39	79	10	0	1
30. Deeply care about the welfare of the individual	48	38	4	1	0	69	51	6	2	1
31. Believe in the institution at all costs	13	53	25	0	0	25	80	24	0	0
32. Encourage creative types even though often in disagreement	22	59	9	1	0	31	84	11	2	1
†33. Appear to make decisions easily	17	59	9	5	1	18	78	17	16	0
34. Appear confident even when in doubt	13	62	14	2	0	13	88	14	12	2
35. View myself and the institution as one	6	36	12	34	3	20	51	13	42	3

4-YEAR									
Effective (N = 221)					Representative (N = 174)				
SA	A	NO	D	SD	SA	A	NO	D	SD
109	97	10	4	1	66	90	9	9	0
35	135	38	12	1	33	104	26	11	0
7	28	13	117	56	9	38	13	86	28
29	141	39	11	1	22	111	33	8	0
10	69	70	62	10	14	55	49	52	4
35	147	27	11	1	27	126	19	2	0
116	92	10	3	0	72	93	9	0	0
32	155	34	0	0	35	122	17	0	0
44	161	11	5	0	33	119	21	1	0
35	135	30	21	0	26	113	18	17	0
29	126	36	29	1	16	116	26	16	0
27	75	19	80	20	18	52	22	68	14

	2-Year									
	Effective (N = 91)					Representative (N = 129)				
Item	SA	A	NO	D	SD	SA	A	NO	D	SD
36. Am often seen as somewhat aloof	2	28	14	39	8	4	48	21	50	6
37. Enjoy stirring things up	3	27	13	38	10	9	33	14	52	21
38. Am rarely viewed as flamboyant	8	69	14	0	0	15	97	17	0	0
39. Appear to enjoy the perquisites of the office	4	49	20	17	1	11	63	28	25	2
40. Smile a lot	21	49	13	8	0	24	71	16	18	0

†Reversed Item

4-Year									
Effective (N = 221)					Representative (N = 174)				
SA	A	NO	D	SD	SA	A	NO	D	SD
8	68	33	94	18	4	53	34	67	16
4	62	35	92	28	8	55	30	62	19
31	151	39	0	0	21	123	30	0	0
9	86	65	56	5	7	73	52	41	1
44	130	27	20	0	40	94	22	17	1

APPENDIX
·*J*·

Comparison of Personal Attitudes and Leadership Styles of Effective Presidents Nominated One, Two, and Three or More Times; Interviewed Presidents; and Representative Presidents

Item	Nominated Once (N = 196)	Nominated Twice (N = 46)	Nominated Three or More (N = 55)	Interviewed (N = 15)	Representative (N = 303)	F Value	p
1. Am sometimes viewed as hard-nosed	2.31	2.35	2.13	2.20	2.23	0.55	.70
2. Believe that the respect of those to be led is essential	1.24	1.17	1.22	1.33	1.31	1.44	.22
3. Believe that an effective leader takes risks	1.39	1.28	1.25	1.20	1.33	1.40	.23
+ 4. Am primarily concerned about being liked	1.89	1.93	1.85	1.67	1.99	2.48	.04*
5. Try to achieve consensus	1.96	1.91	1.84	2.40	2.03	2.44	.05*
6. Believe in organizational structure	1.84	1.74	1.85	2.13	1.75	2.19	.07
7. Believe that the leader should be perceived as self-confident	1.48	1.30	1.51	1.60	1.43	1.45	.22
+ 8. Believe in close collegial relationships	1.82	1.61	1.76	1.67	1.89	3.18	.01**
+ 9. Believe that a leader serves the people	1.56	1.50	1.53	1.67	1.52	0.35	.85
10. Believe in merit pay	1.88	2.07	1.64	1.67	1.95	2.05	.09
11. Am sometimes viewed as assertive	1.82	1.91	1.69	1.80	1.81	0.67	.62

†12. Am rarely in keeping with the status quo	2.10	2.11	2.15	2.00	2.08	0.25	.91
13. Delegate responsibility and authority to subordinates	1.52	1.39	1.49	1.40	1.57	1.52	.19
14. Believe in the value of one-on-one meetings	1.56	1.57	1.53	1.60	1.52	0.19	.94
15. Maintain a measure of mystique	2.89	2.85	2.96	2.93	2.85	0.15	.96
16. Use large social functions to advance the institution	2.21	2.02	2.05	2.27	2.25	0.95	.43
†17. Choose another CEO as a confidant	2.08	2.11	2.04	2.20	2.06	0.35	.85
18. Believe in community involvement	1.50	1.59	1.45	1.47	1.45	0.69	.60
19. Always appear energetic	1.81	1.83	1.71	1.93	1.86	0.59	.67
20. Am often viewed as a loner	3.19	3.20	3.16	3.13	3.14	0.08	.99
†21. Count committee meetings as mistakes	1.96	1.78	1.91	1.73	1.94	1.50	.20
22. Would rather be viewed as a strong leader than a good colleague	2.25	2.43	2.51	2.13	2.19	1.99	.09
23. Accept losses gracefully	2.46	2.26	2.36	2.73	2.54	1.50	.20
24. Tend to work long hours	1.72	1.61	1.65	1.40	1.85	2.64	.03*
†25. Often like people who are different	2.05	2.02	1.93	1.87	1.98	0.85	.49
26. Only occasionally speak spontaneously	3.71	4.17	3.91	4.07	3.50	5.89	.0001***

Item	Nominated Once (N = 196)	Nominated Twice (N = 46)	Nominated Three or More (N = 55)	Interviewed (N = 15)	Representative (N = 303)	F Value	p
27. Am warm and affable	2.27	2.09	2.13	2.20	2.17	0.83	.51
†28. Would rather be influential than professionally admired	2.24	2.24	2.18	2.20	2.14	0.92	.45
29. Dress well	2.00	2.00	1.98	2.13	1.90	1.09	.36
30. Deeply care about the welfare of the individual	1.58	1.59	1.42	1.40	1.61	1.29	.27
31. Believe in the institution at all costs	2.79	3.13	2.98	2.67	2.61	3.12	.01**
32. Encourage creative types even though often in disagreement	1.93	1.83	1.87	1.60	1.92	1.39	.23
†33. Appear to make decisions easily	1.99	1.89	1.96	1.67	1.97	1.55	.19
34. Appear confident even when in doubt	2.22	2.28	2.31	2.00	2.24	0.51	.73
35. View myself and the institution as one	2.90	2.98	3.07	2.93	2.88	0.33	.86
36. Am often seen as somewhat aloof	3.19	3.39	3.22	3.13	3.15	0.56	.69
37. Enjoy stirring things up	3.38	3.30	3.25	3.00	3.24	0.75	.56
38. Am rarely viewed as flamboyant	2.45	2.26	2.35	2.73	2.47	0.97	.42

39. Appear to enjoy the perquisites of the office	2.76	2.65	2.76	3.07	2.67	0.91	.46
40. Smile a lot	2.16	1.89	2.00	2.27	2.16	1.42	.23
Management Style Index	33.64	33.09	32.44	33.67	33.54	0.84	.50
Human Relations Index	20.98	21.04	20.82	20.47	20.56	0.41	.80
Image Index	10.04	9.80	10.15	10.27	9.95	0.23	.92
Social Reference Index	14.53	14.17	14.09	14.47	14.42	0.77	.55
Confidence Index	6.87	7.13	7.09	6.33	6.66	2.35	.05*

*$p < .05$
**$p < .01$
***$p < .0001$
†Reversed Item

APPENDIX
·K·

Comparison of Personal Attitudes and Leadership Styles of Effective and Representative Presidents

Item	EFFECTIVE (N = 312; df = 311)		REPRESENTATIVE (N = 303; df = 302)			
	$\overline{X}$ Response	SD	$\overline{X}$ Response	SD	t	p
1. Am sometimes viewed as hard-nosed	2.28	0.97	2.23	0.97	0.61	.54
2. Believe that the respect of those to be led is essential	1.23	0.42	1.31	0.52	−2.07	.04*
3. Believe that an effective leader takes risks	1.34	0.51	1.33	0.49	0.32	.75
† 4. Am primarily concerned about being liked	1.88	0.52	1.99	0.50	−2.55	.01**
5. Try to achieve consensus	1.96	0.75	2.03	0.63	−1.28	.20

Item	Effective (N = 312; df = 311) X Response	SD	Representative (N = 303; df = 302) X Response	SD	t	p
6. Believe in organizational structure	1.84	0.63	1.75	0.56	1.95	.05*
7. Believe that the leader should be perceived as self-confident	1.46	0.56	1.43	0.55	0.73	.47
† 8. Believe in close collegial relationships	1.77	0.56	1.89	0.57	−2.67	.008**
† 9. Believe that a leader serves the people	1.55	0.62	1.52	0.59	0.61	.54
10. Believe in merit pay	1.85	0.90	1.95	0.91	−1.30	.20
11. Am sometimes viewed as assertive	1.81	0.71	1.81	0.69	−0.02	.99
†12. Am rarely in keeping with the status quo	2.10	0.56	2.08	0.57	0.44	.66
13. Delegate responsibility and authority to subordinates	1.49	0.51	1.57	0.56	−1.86	.06
14. Believe in the value of one-on-one meetings	1.55	0.52	1.52	0.53	0.70	.49
15. Maintain a measure of mystique	2.90	1.13	2.85	1.13	0.57	.57
16. Use large social functions to advance the institution	2.16	0.95	2.25	0.99	−1.24	.22
†17. Choose another CEO as a confidant	2.08	0.58	2.06	0.55	0.53	.60
18. Believe in community involvement	1.50	0.63	1.45	0.57	1.20	.23
19. Always appear energetic	1.80	0.73	1.86	0.77	−1.00	.32
20. Am often viewed as a loner	3.19	1.07	3.14	1.07	0.51	.61
†21. Count committee meetings as mistakes	1.92	0.54	1.94	0.57	−0.46	.65
22. Would rather be viewed as a strong leader than a good colleague	2.32	0.93	2.19	0.89	1.75	.08
23. Accept losses gracefully	2.43	0.88	2.54	0.96	−1.50	.13
24. Tend to work long hours	1.68	0.76	1.85	0.81	−2.78	.006**
†25. Often like people who are different	2.01	0.57	1.98	0.58	0.77	.44

Item	Effective (N = 312; df = 311)		Representative (N = 303; df = 302)			
	X̄ Response	SD	X̄ Response	SD	t	p
26. Only occasionally speak spontaneously	3.83	1.02	3.50	1.11	3.90	.0001***
27. Am warm and affable	2.21	0.77	2.17	0.75	0.65	.52
†28. Would rather be influential than professionally admired	2.23	0.60	2.14	0.58	1.80	.07
29. Dress well	2.00	0.71	1.90	0.60	1.94	.05*
30. Deeply care about the welfare of the individual	1.54	0.64	1.61	0.65	−1.20	.23
31. Believe in the institution at all costs	2.87	1.11	2.61	1.15	2.80	.005**
32. Encourage creative types even though often in disagreement	1.89	0.58	1.92	0.62	−0.68	.50
†33. Appear to make decisions easily	1.96	0.54	1.97	0.51	−0.36	.72
34. Appear confident even when in doubt	2.23	0.82	2.24	0.78	−0.11	.91
35. View myself and the institution as one	2.95	1.20	2.88	1.19	0.63	.53
36. Am often seen as somewhat aloof	3.22	1.07	3.15	1.05	0.89	.38
37. Enjoy stirring things up	3.33	1.08	3.24	1.17	1.02	.31
38. Am rarely viewed as flamboyant	2.42	0.93	2.47	0.96	−0.64	.52
39. Appear to enjoy the perquisites of the office	2.76	0.92	2.67	0.92	1.17	.24
40. Smile a lot	2.10	0.83	2.16	0.90	−0.80	.42
Management Style Index	33.35	4.89	35.54	4.40	−0.50	.62
Human Relations Index	20.94	3.89	20.56	4.12	1.16	.25
Image Index	10.04	2.37	9.95	2.32	0.45	.65
Social Reference Index	14.39	1.94	14.42	1.83	−0.19	.85
Confidence Index	6.92	1.37	6.66	1.52	2.23	.03*

*$p < .05$
**$p < .01$
***$p < .0001$
†Reversed Item

Comparison of Personal Attitudes and Leadership Styles of Presidents Nominated One Time and Those Nominated Two or More Times

	One Nomination (N = 198; df = 197)		Two or More Nominations (N = 114; df = 113)			
Item	X̄ Response	SD	X̄ Response	SD	t	p
1. Am sometimes viewed as hard-nosed	2.30	1.00	2.24	0.91	0.54	.59
2. Believe that the respect of those to be led is essential	1.24	0.43	1.22	0.42	0.36	.72
3. Believe that an effective leader takes risks	1.39	0.52	1.26	0.50	2.09	.04*
† 4. Am primarily concerned about being liked	1.88	0.53	1.88	0.50	0.11	.91
5. Try to achieve consensus	1.96	0.78	1.94	0.68	0.30	.77
6. Believe in organizational structure	1.83	0.64	1.86	0.62	−0.42	.67
7. Believe that the leader should be perceived as self-confident	1.48	0.56	1.44	0.56	0.62	.53
† 8. Believe in close collegial relationships	1.82	0.54	1.68	0.58	2.05	.04*
† 9. Believe that a leader serves the people	1.57	0.62	1.55	0.61	0.54	.59
10. Believe in merit pay	1.88	0.89	1.81	0.92	0.68	.50
11. Am sometimes viewed as assertive	1.82	0.70	1.80	0.73	0.24	.81
†12. Am rarely in keeping with the status quo	2.10	0.57	2.11	0.55	−0.06	.95
13. Delegate responsibility and authority to subordinates	1.52	.51	1.45	0.50	1.14	.26
14. Believe in the value of one-on-one meetings	1.56	.51	1.54	0.55	0.27	.79
15. Maintain a measure of mystique	2.88	1.14	2.93	1.13	−0.34	.73
16. Use large social functions to advance the institution	2.20	.93	2.09	0.98	0.98	.33
†17. Choose another CEO as a confidant	2.09	0.57	2.08	0.60	0.10	.92
18. Believe in community involvement	1.49	0.65	1.52	0.58	−0.31	.76

Item	ONE NOMINATION ($N = 198$; $df = 197$)		TWO OR MORE NOMINATIONS ($N = 114$; $df = 113$)			
	$\overline{X}$ Response	SD	$\overline{X}$ Response	SD	t	p
19. Always appear energetic	1.81	0.74	1.79	0.72	0.22	.83
20. Am often viewed as a loner	3.20	1.06	3.17	1.08	0.24	.81
†21. Count committee meetings as mistakes	1.96	0.54	1.84	0.53	1.87	.06
22. Would rather be viewed as a strong leader than a good colleague	2.24	0.91	2.45	0.96	−1.87	.06
23. Accept losses gracefully	2.46	0.86	2.38	0.93	0.79	.43
24. Tend to work long hours	1.71	0.75	1.61	0.77	1.10	.27
†25. Often like people who are different	2.05	0.55	1.96	0.60	1.33	.19
26. Only occasionally speak spontaneously	3.72	1.04	4.03	0.95	−2.57	.01**
27. Am warm and affable	2.26	0.77	2.13	0.76	1.40	.16
†28. Would rather be influential than professionally admired	2.24	0.61	2.21	0.57	0.38	.70
29. Dress well	1.99	0.72	2.02	0.69	−0.27	.79
30. Deeply care about the welfare of the individual	1.58	0.67	1.48	0.60	1.30	.20
31. Believe in the institution at all costs	2.77	1.11	3.04	1.10	−2.06	.04*
32. Encourage creative types even though often in disagreement	1.93	0.61	1.82	0.52	1.73	.08
†33. Appear to make decisions easily	1.98	0.51	1.90	0.59	1.28	.20
34. Appear confident even when in doubt	2.22	0.81	2.26	0.83	−0.48	.63
35. View myself and the institution as one	2.89	1.17	3.04	1.26	−1.10	.27
36. Am often seen as somewhat aloof	3.19	1.09	3.28	1.05	−0.74	.46
37. Enjoy stirring things up	3.39	1.04	3.23	1.15	1.26	.21
38. Am rarely viewed as flamboyant	2.45	0.95	2.35	0.89	0.95	.34

Item	Three or More Nominations ($N = 67$; $df = 66$)		One or Two Nominations ($N = 245$; $df = 244$)			
	$\overline{X}$ Response	SD	$\overline{X}$ Response	SD	t	p
39. Appear to enjoy the perquisites of the office	2.75	0.91	2.76	0.95	−0.10	.92
40. Smile a lot	2.16	0.87	2.00	0.74	1.61	.11
Management Style Index	33.60	4.92	32.91	4.83	1.20	.23
Human Relations Index	20.96	3.99	20.90	3.72	0.12	.90
Image Index	10.02	2.35	10.07	2.43	−0.20	.84
Social Reference Index	14.52	1.90	14.18	1.99	1.52	.13
Confidence Index	6.85	1.40	7.04	1.31	−1.18	.24

$*p < .05$
$**p < .01$
†Reversed Item

APPENDIX
·M·

Comparison of Personal Attitudes and Leadership Styles of Presidents Nominated Three or More Times and Those Nominated Less Than Three Times

Item	THREE OR MORE NOMINATIONS ($N = 67$; $df = 66$)		ONE OR TWO NOMINATIONS ($N = 245$; $df = 244$)			
	$\overline{X}$ Response	SD	$\overline{X}$ Response	SD	t	p
1. Am sometimes viewed as hard-nosed	2.18	0.92	2.30	0.98	−0.92	.36
2. Believe that the respect of those to be led is essential	1.25	0.44	1.22	0.42	0.50	.62
3. Believe that an effective leader takes risks	1.25	0.44	1.37	0.53	−1.61	.11
† 4. Am primarily concerned about being liked	1.84	0.48	1.89	0.53	−0.81	.42
5. Try to achieve consensus	1.93	0.70	1.96	0.76	−0.37	.71
6. Believe in organizational structure	1.93	0.66	1.82	0.62	1.25	.21
7. Believe that the leader should be perceived as self-confident	1.54	0.61	1.44	0.55	1.20	.23
† 8. Believe in close collegial relationships	1.75	0.61	1.78	0.55	−0.38	.71
† 9. Believe that a leader serves the people	1.55	0.61	1.55	0.62	0.01	.99
10. Believe in merit pay	1.64	0.81	1.91	0.92	−2.17	.03*
11. Am sometimes viewed as assertive	1.73	0.62	1.83	0.73	−1.04	.30
†12. Am rarely in keeping with the status quo	2.11	0.59	2.10	0.56	0.28	.78
13. Delegate responsibility and authority to subordinates	1.49	.50	1.49	0.51	0.04	.97
14. Believe in the value of one-on-one meetings	1.54	.53	1.56	0.52	−0.30	.76
15. Maintain a measure of mystique	3.01	1.09	2.87	1.14	0.93	.35
16. Use large social functions to advance the institution	2.12	1.01	2.17	0.94	−0.37	.72
†17. Choose another CEO as a confidant	2.07	0.59	2.09	0.58	−0.14	.89
18. Believe in community involvement	1.48	0.59	1.51	0.64	−0.38	.71

Item	THREE OR MORE NOMINATIONS ($N = 67$; $df = 66$)		ONE OR TWO NOMINATIONS ($N = 245$; $df = 244$)			
	$\overline{X}$ Response	SD	$\overline{X}$ Response	SD	t	p
19. Always appear energetic	1.78	0.79	1.81	0.71	−0.32	.75
20. Am often viewed as a loner	3.16	1.04	3.19	1.08	−0.19	.85
†21. Count committee meetings as mistakes	1.88	0.48	1.93	0.55	−0.62	.54
22. Would rather be viewed as a strong leader than a good colleague	2.43	1.03	2.29	0.91	1.14	.25
23. Accept losses gracefully	2.42	0.94	2.43	0.87	−0.12	.90
24. Tend to work long hours	1.63	0.79	1.69	0.75	−0.60	.55
†25. Often like people who are different	1.90	0.58	2.04	0.57	−1.90	.06
26. Only occasionally speak spontaneously	3.93	1.02	3.81	1.02	0.84	.40
27. Am warm and affable	2.16	0.83	2.22	0.75	−0.57	.57
†28. Would rather be influential than professionally admired	2.19	0.56	2.24	0.61	−0.52	.60
29. Dress well	2.03	0.72	2.00	0.70	0.35	.73
30. Deeply care about the welfare of the individual	1.42	0.61	1.58	0.65	−1.83	.07
31. Believe in the institution at all costs	3.00	1.03	2.83	1.13	1.12	.26
32. Encourage creative types even though often in disagreement	1.82	0.58	1.91	0.59	−1.11	.27
†33. Appear to make decisions easily	1.93	0.61	1.96	0.52	−0.51	.61
34. Appear confident even when in doubt	2.27	0.91	2.22	0.79	0.39	.70
35. View myself and the institution as one	3.12	1.30	2.90	1.17	1.34	.18
36. Am often seen as somewhat aloof	3.22	1.04	3.22	1.08	0.02	.98
37. Enjoy stirring things up	3.15	1.16	3.38	1.06	−1.55	.12
38. Am rarely viewed as flamboyant	2.43	0.89	2.41	0.94	0.16	.87

Item	Three or More Nominations ($N = 67$; $df = 66$)		One or Two Nominations ($N = 245$; $df = 244$)			
	$\bar{X}$ Response	SD	$\bar{X}$ Response	SD	t	p
39. Appear to enjoy the perquisites of the office	2.84	0.98	2.73	0.91	0.79	.43
40. Smile a lot	2.07	0.74	2.11	0.85	−0.28	.78
Management Style Index	32.81	4.92	33.50	4.88	−1.03	.31
Human Relations Index	20.84	3.88	20.97	3.90	−0.25	.81
Image Index	10.30	2.70	9.96	2.28	1.02	.31
Social Reference Index	14.21	1.81	14.44	1.97	−0.88	.38
Confidence Index	7.04	1.25	6.89	1.41	0.82	.41

$*p < .05$
†Reversed Item

APPENDIX

·*N*·

Comparison of Personal Attitudes and Leadership Styles of Interviewed Presidents and Those Nominated One or More Times

Item	INTERVIEWED (N = 15; df = 14)		ONE OR MORE NOMINATIONS (N = 297; df = 296)			
	$\overline{X}$ Response	SD	$\overline{X}$ Response	SD	t	p
1. Am sometimes viewed as hard-nosed	2.20	0.94	2.28	0.97	−0.31	.76
2. Believe that the respect of those to be led is essential	1.33	0.49	1.23	0.42	0.96	.34
3. Believe that an effective leader takes risks	1.20	0.41	1.35	0.52	−1.10	.27
† 4. Am primarily concerned about being liked	1.67	0.62	1.89	0.52	−1.64	.10
5. Try to achieve consensus	2.40	0.91	1.93	0.73	2.38	.02*
6. Believe in organizational structure	2.13	0.83	1.82	0.62	1.85	.06
7. Believe that the leader should be perceived as self-confident	1.60	0.83	1.46	0.54	0.66	.52
† 8. Believe in close collegial relationships	1.67	0.62	1.77	0.56	−0.73	.47
† 9. Believe that a leader serves the people	1.67	0.62	1.55	0.62	0.73	.46
10. Believe in merit pay	1.67	0.90	1.86	0.90	−0.82	.41
11. Am sometimes viewed as assertive	1.80	0.68	1.81	0.71	−0.06	.95
†12. Am rarely in keeping with the status quo	2.00	0.65	2.11	0.56	−0.72	.47
13. Delegate responsibility and authority to subordinates	1.40	0.51	1.49	0.51	−0.71	.48
14. Believe in the value of one-on-one meetings	1.60	0.51	1.55	0.52	0.34	.73
15. Maintain a measure of mystique	2.93	1.10	2.90	1.14	0.11	.91
16. Use large social functions to advance the institution	2.27	1.28	2.15	0.93	0.46	.65
†17. Choose another CEO as a confidant	2.20	0.56	2.08	0.58	0.80	.42
18. Believe in community involvement	1.47	0.74	1.51	0.62	−0.23	.82

Item	INTERVIEWED (N = 15; df = 14)		ONE OR MORE NOMINATIONS (N = 297; df = 296)			
	$\overline{X}$ Response	SD	$\overline{X}$ Response	SD	t	p
19. Always appear energetic	1.93	0.88	1.79	0.72	0.72	.47
20. Am often viewed as a loner	3.13	1.13	3.19	1.07	−0.19	.85
†21. Count committee meetings as mistakes	1.73	0.46	1.90	0.54	−1.35	.17
22. Would rather be viewed as a strong leader than a good colleague	2.13	1.13	2.33	0.93	−0.78	.44
23. Accept losses gracefully	2.73	1.03	2.41	0.87	1.37	.17
24. Tend to work long hours	1.40	0.83	1.69	0.75	−1.45	.15
†25. Often like people who are different	1.87	0.64	2.02	0.57	−1.01	.31
26. Only occasionally speak spontaneously	4.07	0.80	3.82	1.03	0.91	.36
27. Am warm and affable	2.20	1.01	2.21	0.76	−0.06	.95
†28. Would rather be influential than professionally admired	2.20	0.56	2.22	0.60	−0.18	.85
29. Dress well	2.13	0.74	2.00	0.70	0.73	.47
30. Deeply care about the welfare of the individual	1.40	0.51	1.55	0.65	−0.89	.37
31. Believe in the institution at all costs	2.67	1.23	2.87	1.10	−0.71	.48
32. Encourage creative types even though often in disagreement	1.60	0.51	1.91	0.59	−1.99	.05*
†33. Appear to make decisions easily	1.67	0.62	1.97	0.54	−2.12	.03*
34. Appear confident even when in doubt	2.00	0.76	2.25	0.82	−1.14	.26
35. View myself and the institution as one	2.93	1.33	2.95	1.20	−0.04	.97
36. Am often seen as somewhat aloof	3.13	1.06	3.23	1.07	−0.32	.75
37. Enjoy stirring things up	3.00	1.36	3.35	1.07	−1.21	.23
38. Am rarely viewed as flamboyant	2.73	1.03	2.40	0.93	1.35	.18

	INTERVIEWED $(N = 15;$ $df = 14)$		ONE OR MORE NOMINATIONS $(N = 297;$ $df = 296)$			
Item	$\overline{X}$ Response	SD	$\overline{X}$ Response	SD	t	p
39. Appear to enjoy the perquisites of the office	3.07	0.88	2.74	0.92	1.33	.18
40. Smile a lot	2.27	0.88	2.09	0.83	0.80	.42
Management Style Index	33.67	5.39	33.33	4.88	0.25	.79
Human Relations Index	20.46	3.02	20.96	3.93	−0.48	.63
Image Index	10.27	2.79	10.02	2.36	0.39	.70
Social Reference Index	14.47	1.30	14.39	1.96	0.14	.88
Confidence Index	6.33	1.68	6.95	1.35	−1.71	.08

$*p < .05$
†Reversed Items

Index